あきらめの英語

【あるがままの国際理解教育】

島田将夫・吉村雅仁 著

大学教育出版

はじめに

　「国際理解教育」と教科目としての「英語」。英語教育関係者や英語学習者は、この2つの関係をどのように捉えているのでしょうか。「国際理解教育」は、「英語」の中で行われるものなのか、「英語」がその一部を担うだけなのか、あるいは「英語」とは別に考える方がよいのか。当然ながらこの両者の関係は、国際理解の定義や英語という言語の捉え方によって様々に変化します。

　まず、国際理解＝「異文化理解」、英語＝「米・英国等のいわゆる英語国の言語」といった、それぞれ最も狭い見方をするならば、「国際理解教育」は、他国ないしは他民族文化の紹介とそれと対比させた自文化の認識を目指す教育ということになり、教科目としての「英語」教育の目的は、英語圏の言語および文化を体得させ付随的に自国の言語や文化にも新しい視点を与えることとなります。

　この場合ですと、英語教育に携わる教師だけでなく英語の学習者にとっても、教科目としての「英語」と「国際理解教育」との関係はもちろん、「英語」の目的や内容も極めて明確なものになると言ってよいでしょう。すなわち、教科目としての「英語」は「国際理解教育」の一部を担うものであり、目標とする英語は英米人とのコミュニケーションを可能にする（いわゆる「標準」）英語となります。教材として扱う内容も英語圏の文化そしてそれと対比させた自国の文化に限定されてきます。

　一方、国際理解や英語を広義に捉えるとどうなるでしょう。近年の学校現場で一般化しつつある国際理解あるいは「国際理解教育」の概念はこの広義の捉え方をしており、人権教育、環境教育、平和教育、多文化教育、異文化理解教育、開発教育、帰国子女教育、国際交流・国際協力などを含む非常に広い領域を指すと考えられます。さらに英語についても、「国際共通語」ないしは「国際便宜語」としての地位を強化し続けている現状から、英語は「米・英国等のいわゆる英語国の言語」というより「世界（共通）語」であるという認識が徐々

に広がりつつあります。この認識、考え方は、英語を英米文化から切り離し、コミュニケーションのための単なる道具として捉えるものであり、「国際英語論」という名で呼ばれることもあります。

　それぞれのこの広い定義を組み合わせて両者の関係を見ると、2つの両極端な考え方ができます。1つは、「国際理解教育」の本質的な部分はむしろ「社会科」や「総合的な学習」で扱われるものであり、「英語」が貢献できるとすれば、せいぜい情報収集・伝達、交流、協力のための道具、技術、手段の1つを提供するのみというものです。「英語」の狭い定義の1つの柱である「英米文化理解」を排除するのですから、「国際理解教育」の中で占めることのできる「異文化理解教育」の役割すら消えてしまうというわけです。

　もう一方の極端な考え方は、「英語」が「国際理解教育」の非常に幅広い領域のほとんどすべてにおいて重要な役割を担うことができるとするものです。英語という道具が、国際あるいは異文化間コミュニケーションの最も効率のよい手段として、幸か不幸か広く普及してしまったがゆえに、情報受信・発信、国際交流・協力の道具としての英語の強さは他言語と比べ群を抜いています。教科目としての「英語」の教材を考えた場合、「国際理解教育」にかかわる情報を集めるのに事欠くことはまずありません。また、単に道具としての役割だけではなく、「国際理解教育」の本質的な問題をも「英語」は扱うことが可能となります。英語の世界的普及から生じた結果ではありますが、英語による世界中の膨大かつ多様な資料の中には、たとえば人権問題や環境問題などの「告発」が数多く存在します。いわば、「国際理解教育」の範疇に入る問題を告発する「生の声」の宝庫なのです。第3者（たとえば翻訳者）を通さず、「生の声」を聞き、場合によっては「疑似体験」まで可能にする教科目として「英語」は最適の科目ということもできます。

　本書は、基本的に両者の広義の定義を組み合わせ、教科目としての「英語」が「国際理解教育」の本質的な役割を担えるという立場をとります。広い意味での「国際理解教育」に資するであろうと著者が考える情報を、日本語、英語を織り交ぜて示してあるだけでなく、人権問題等を訴える「生の声」も載せています。

　本論に入る前に、もう1つ付け加えておくことがあります。本書を読み進め

る際の心構えというか態度の問題です。上で述べたこととある意味矛盾すると感じられるかもしれませんが、著者の基本的立場、すなわち英語を広義に単なる道具と捉えること、そして広い意味での国際理解、このような考え方そのものの限界をも同時に考えていただきたいと思います。「基本的」と付け加えたのはこの理由によるものです。そもそも「外（国）語を教える・学ぶことはどういうことなのか」、「国際理解は可能なのか」、という最も根本的な問題を常に頭の片隅にでも置きながら本書を読んでいただければ、著者の意図をよりよく察していただけるのではないかと期待しています。

　私たちは皆、多くの根本的な問題を、しばしば「常識」とか「あたりまえ」ということにして、見過ごしてしまいがちです。もっとも、自分の身の回りに生じるあらゆる「常識」に対していちいち神経を尖らせていては疲れ果ててしまうことも確かです。しかし、自分の「常識」が覆される経験は、自分の価値観や場合によっては人生をも変えてしまうほど大きな意味を持つことがあります。それは、強い関心、衝撃、感動、あるいは失望や嫌悪感をもたらすものであるかもしれません。いずれにせよ、そのような体験は、何かを丸暗記することなどに比べて遥かに何かを「学んだ」と感じられるものではないでしょうか。「外（国）語」教育、「国際理解教育」に限らず、少なくとも公教育の教科目のいずれにもその種の「楽しみ」が盛り込まれることを私たちは望んでいますし、自らも実践できればよいと感じています。本書がその目的を達成するのに少しでも役立てば幸いに思います。

　読者の皆さんの「常識」をはじめに確認していただく意味も込めて、ここで2点注釈を付けておきます。1つは本書のカバーにある挿し絵です。この肖像は、米国の宗教週刊誌、*National Catholic Reporter* 新千年紀特別号（西暦1999年12月発行）の表紙に採用されたものです。これは誰の肖像だと思われるでしょうか。答えは、「イエス・キリスト」です。「え？　イエスは白い肌、金髪に青い眼じゃなかったの？」とまでいかなくとも、「イエスは白人では？」というのが、多くの読者の反応ではないでしょうか。

　もう1つは、本書中の年号の前に頻繁に付け加えられた「西暦」です。「分かりきっているのにくどい」と思われる方もおられるかもしれませんが、これも「常識」を今一度見つめ直していただくために故意にしたことです。あたかも

「グローバル・スタンダード」のように使用される「西暦」はいくつもある時間軸の1つにすぎません。暦にはほとんどの場合その背景に宗教があると考えられます。と言われると気がつく方も多いでしょう。「西暦」は「キリスト教（グレゴリオ）暦」のことです。ちなみにキリスト教暦2001年1月1日は、イスラム暦1421年10月5日、ユダヤ暦5761年4月6日、そして平成13年1月1日、ついでに皇紀2661年1月1日となります。「それでも世界ではキリスト教徒が圧倒的多数派だ」と言われる方についでに申し上げると、キリスト教徒の人口はある推計によると世界中で12～13億人、世界の人口約60億のおよそ5分の1。確かに多数ではあるけれど、世界の残り5分の4はキリスト教徒ではないということになります。中にはイスラム教徒の人口の方が大きいという推計もあります。案外「常識」というものがあてにならないと感じられる方もおられるのではないでしょうか？

　最後に、本書の記述が特に英語教育界では現在少数派の言説を視座に据えているにもかかわらず、快く出版をお引き受け下さり、著者二人を最後まで温かく見守ってくださった大学教育出版の佐藤守氏には、心から感謝いたします。

平成13年7月1日

島田　将夫
吉村　雅仁

あきらめの英語
――あるがままの国際理解教育――

目　次

はじめに　i

序　章 ………………………………………………………………… 1

第1章　明らめのすすめ ………………………………………… 9
　　　明らめのすすめ　9
　　　語学を明らめよう　11
　　　言語と文化とは一体　12
　　　「total commitment」は狂気　21
　　　ここは日本、日本語でしゃべれ　25
　　　世界人権宣言　27
　　　世界言語権宣言　35
　　　英語を明らめよう　59

第2章　明らめの試み ………………………………………… 62
　　　エル・ハジ・マリク・エル・シャバズ　62
　　　黒人民族主義（black nationalism）　67
　　　自衛（self-defense）　80
　　　人権（human rights）　90
　　　「あるがまま」のマルコムX演説　96
　　　「黒人大衆へのメッセージ」　97
　　　「OAAUの基本方針と目的」　111

第3章　あるがままの国際理解 ……………………………… 134
　　　「国際理解教育」の実践者　134
　　　あるがままの「人権国家」　135
　　　国家を越えて　141
　　　あるがままの国際理解教育　141
　　　国際理解（教育）を明らめる　148

第4章　暗誦のすすめ……………………………………………151
　こだわり（分別）のない「まるごと」　*151*
　文章まるごと楽しむ　*153*
　「文の成り立ち」……自然に与えられた能力を活かそう　*154*
　再構成とメモ　*156*
　「小話」の再構成、模範演習　*158*
　文章まるごと暗誦のすすめ　*184*

付録　マルコムＸのスピーチの暗誦例 ……………………………186

　引用・参考文献　*190*

序　章

　あまりにも恵まれたことに、筆者は平和な環境で生まれ育ち今日に至りました。戦乱の恐怖の中で「命さえ助かれば！」と思うような経験をしたことは一度もありません。それどころか、飢餓に苦しんだり、居所を追われたり、着衣に不足したことすら経験がないのです。地上では毎日、戦禍の犠牲になったり迫害や圧制や飢餓に苦しむ多くの人々がいると伝えられているにもかかわらず、平和な経済大国である日本で捨てるほど余りある物資を何不自由なく享受し、ボーッ（漫然）と暮らしてきました。この点におきましては、昭和36年（西暦1961年）の日本国に生まれ、日本国の主権の及ぶ国土で日本国民として生きることになった縁（えにし）は、幸運中の幸運であったと感じています。しかしながら、このような未曾有の平和と物質的豊かさの中にドップリと漬かり込んでしまったがゆえに、筆者は他国家や他民族との紛争というものが実感としてとらえることがまったくできないのです。無くなれば直ちに人間が生命を維持できなくなるものとして、気圧（や重力）や温度や空気（酸素）や水や光などの地球環境がありますが、あたかも無尽蔵のごとく「無償」で手に入ることのできる通常の生活では、それらの貴重さを我々がほとんど認識できずにいるのと似ています（近年は環境問題などで多少認識されてきましたが……）。

　安全保障を自ら獲得し、それを維持する苦難を経験したことのない筆者には「国際利害」の調節とはいかなるものなのかが実感としてまったく把握できないのです。すなわち、何をどうすれば紛争が回避され、そしてそれを持続できるのか、まったく分からないのです。本書において、これほどまでに完璧に、平和の意味がまったく理解できない著者が、国際秩序の達成と維持の礎の1つとして一般に多くの人々が重要視している「国際理解」、そしてその最も有効な手段の1つと信じられている「英語の習得（語学）」について問いかけることを、まずはお許し下さい。

日本国憲法の前文では「日本国民は、恒久の平和を念願し、人間相互の関係を支配する崇高な理想を深く自覚するのであって、平和を愛する諸国民の公正と信義に信頼して、我らの安全と生存を保持しようと決意した」とあり、それについて「日本国民は、国家の名誉にかけ、全力をあげてこの崇高な理想と目的を達成することを誓う」とあります。単純に換言しますと、"（国家間の政治レベルであれ私人間のレベルであれ）日本の国是は「平和」、日本の存立基盤は「国際平和」にあり、それは「国際理解」によって達成され維持されるべく全力を尽くせ"ということになると思います。すなわち、「平和」の存続に資する「国際理解」に貢献することは善であると公認し、日本国民の価値体系に「国際理解は善である」という価値観を組み込むことにしているのです。

さて近年、日本の公教育（学校教育）における外国語教育、実質的には英語教育が、この「国際理解」そしてその手段としての「コミュニケーション能力の育成」を大義とする旗幟をいよいよ鮮明にしてまいりました。平成14年4月1日から施行される中学校学習指導要領では、外国語の目標は「外国語を通じて、言語や文化に対する理解を深め、積極的にコミュニケーションを図ろうとする態度の育成を図り、聞くことや話すことなどの実践的コミュニケーション能力の基礎を養う」とされています。そして、それを実現するための教材に関しては「広い視野から国際理解を深め、国際社会に生きる日本人としての自覚を高めるとともに、国際協調の精神を養うのに役立つこと」と「言語や文化に対する関心を高め、これらを尊重する態度を育てるとともに、豊かな心情を育てるのに役立つこと」と「世界や我が国の生活や文化についての理解を深め、国際的な視野を広げ、公正な判断力を養うのに役立つこと」とに配慮する必要を説いています。要約すると「「国際理解」に資するために、英語によるコミュニケーション能力を養成せよ」となります。

上述のとおり日本国は「国際理解」を善と憲法で定める国家ですので、公教育の主要教科の1つである英語教育が「国際理解」を大義とすることによって「正義」の科目となり得るのです。そして、善・悪、正義・不正義、役に立つ・役に立たないが明確にされ、大義を得た英語教育界では、その成員である英語教師の多くが、「国際理解」を「善」とし、その実現に役に立つ「英語コミュニケーション能力」が必要である、という価値観に学習者を同化させることが平

和に貢献する「正義」の実践であるとの使命感をますます増大させているように思われます。

ところで、英語教育界で多用される「コミュニケーション」とは何でしょうか？　英語でしたら、「society（社会）」と「socialize（社会（同）化）」の関係のごとく、「community」と「communicate」は関係が深く、「communicate」することが「communication」なのだとうかがえます。すなわち、「community」は「共同体（他人と共有の状態）」ですので「communicate」は「共同体に同化する（他人と共有する）」という意味となるのです。ですから「コミュニケーション」とは「伝達」や「意思疎通」などの訳語で知られますが、「共同体に同化する」ことを前提とする「意思疎通」なのです。そもそも、人と人との「意思疎通」が達成されるにはお互いの価値観が共有されていなければなりませんから、当然と言うべきことであります。ですから、ある人（共同体）とある人（共同体）との「コミュニケーション」が成立したとは、意思疎通がされたことと表裏一体に当事者の価値観が（多くの場合どちらか一方に）同化したことを意味するわけです。

したがって上述の指導要領での、英語で「積極的にコミュニケーションを図ろうとする態度の育成を図り」とはとりもなおさず、「英語を話す人々の価値観に同化する態度を育成する」ことにほかならないのではないでしょうか？　そしてこのこと自体が善の価値とするならば、たとえば「大人しく、寡黙で、自己主張せず、独立した自由な人格」を持つ学習者は「だめな人間」と「分別」してしまいます。なぜならば、「活発で、よく発言し、自己主張ができ、他人との競争に勝つべく鋭意努力する人格」を善しとするのがおおむね英語を母語とする共同体に属する人々の価値観だからです。この価値観に同化しない限り英語母語話者とのコミュニケーションは大概において成立し得ないからです。

そもそも人間の認識は「分別」を基盤にしていることが、科学と呼ばれる人間の「分別」の活動による成果として明らかになってきました。そのことが明らかになってきた科学の分野の1つが、言語学であります。ことばの2大特徴の1つをごく簡単に言い切ってしまえば、「ことばは自然を「分別」する人間の能力（限界）の1つ」というように「分別」されています。すなわち、ある1つの言語は、その言語共同体の成員がおおむね共有する価値観の体系というこ

とになります。なぜならば、価値観とは、たとえば、善・悪や正義・不正義や美・醜などの対立概念による自然の事象の「分別」の結果であります。そして幸か不幸か、自然は1つであるにもかかわらず、人間が分別した善・悪や正義・不正義や美・醜などの価値観は、言語共同体ごとに違いが見られるのです。もっと極言すれば、人間は千差万別、一人ひとりの価値観はすべて違うのです。ただ言語共同体ごとに一般的傾向が見られるに過ぎません。それがその共同体ごとの常識・非常識なのです。俗にしばしば、音楽に国境はないとか、美にことばはいらないなどと言われるのを聞いたことがありますが、ベートーベンの『歓喜』が騒音にしか聞こえない人も実際に多くいますし、ダビンチの『モナリザ』がもしも原野に落ちていたら、貨幣価値（これもことば的「分別」が生み出す価値）自体とそれが貨幣価値的に高価なものであることを知らない限り、それを踏みつけて通る人だってたくさんいると思います。単純に言い切れば、対立概念による「分別」の装置である人間のことばは、自然のある一面をある概念で「分別」すれば、その面に対して無限に可能である他の「分別」の一切を認識できなくさせてしまうのです。

　この人間の特性はいろいろな意味であまねく人間にとって幸なのか不幸なのかよく分からないのですが、少なくとも言えることは、「コミュニケーション」の手段としてことばは非常に不完全なものであります。本書第1章ではこれらのことを踏まえ、「コミュニケーション」を目的とする外語（特に英語）の学習（「語学」）がいかなるものであるかについて述べています。

　それにしても、そもそも「国際理解」とは何でしょうか？　「国家やその他の共同体どうし、もしくはおのおのの共同体からの成員どうしの理解や意思疎通」というところが一般的な定義だと思いますし、仮にそうします。しかし、そこに国家や共同体や言語の障壁があったとしても、人間一人ひとりの理解、「人際理解」と本質的には何ら変わりがないのではないでしょうか？

　著者は、この「人と人との理解」こそが「可不可一貫」（この概念について詳しくは『荘子』をお読み下さい）であると観ます。「可不可一貫」とは著者流に咀嚼し極言いたしますと、「対立概念として『分別』されたもの（事象）は本来『無分別』な実在であり、実在するのはそこにある1つの自然のみである」ということです。したがって、「人と人とが理解」し合えたか（可）そうでないか

（不可）というのは、人間がつける対立概念（ことば）による「分別」であって、実際に「人と人とが理解」し合えたか（可）そうでないか（不可）というのは「分別」がつけられるものでなく、実在するのはそこにいる「人と人」のみなのです。実際、親子でもいいし、恋人どうし、身近な人どうしでも、そもそも「人と人とが理解」し合ったという判定をどうしてつけられるのでしょうか？「心がうち溶け合った」、「心が1つになった」などと感じることがあっても、それは当人どうしの「誤解」によるものであることがどうして否定できるでしょうか？　第一、自分でも自分を十分に理解することが、人間にはできるのでしょうか？

　このような意味において、「国際理解」などという理念はただの妄想、少なくとも「人知の及ばざる」ものなのです。そして「人知の及ばざる」ものに対処するには、「こだわるな」という「明らめ」の態度が最も重要なのです。そもそも、自然と人為とを人間が勝手に「分別」したりしますが、本来は人間も自然の一部ですから、その自然の一部である人間の行いとその結果としての人為もすべて自然の一部です。能力の制限された目や耳や鼻や舌や皮膚などの感覚器官を通して得られた情報を非常に不確実なことば的な「分別」をもって知覚する自然存在ですから、当然人間も自然の力に支配されています。その制限を超えたことにこだわりを持っても意味のないことであります。

　以上の意味において、著者は本書の中で、英語教育における「国際理解」などという妄念に「こだわるな」と主張したいのです。人間はそもそも、「半ば社会的な動物であり、半ば孤独な動物である」とバートランド・ラッセルも定義するように、完全な共同体化（communicate）はできない反面、完全に孤立もできない存在のようです。それぞれ生まれ持った内面の個性に合わせて、社会と孤独の「中庸」（ちょうど"いい加減"なところ）を実践するのが最も幸福な（自然に適合した）生き方のようです。ですからもしも、英語教育においてあくまでも誰一人その理を知り得ない「コミュニケーション能力」や「国際理解」にこだわり、それによって学習者を「分別」していくことは、学習者の自然のうちの人間性を破壊する行為にほかならないからです。

　親の願望（価値観）を無理やり押し付けて、不幸になった子供がたくさんいるがごとく、国家の思惑や大計（価値観）を無理やり押し付けて、不幸になっ

た国民がたくさんいるのではないでしょうか？　そもそも常識・非常識（価値観）は時代の趨勢とともに変化します。つい50数年前までは「鬼畜米英」や「贅沢は敵・欲しがりません勝つまでは」や「英語＝敵性語」を常識として国民に押し付け、その価値観への同化により国民と非国民を「分別」していた国家が、今は「国際理解」や「内需拡大」や「英語コミュニケーション能力」という価値によって同様に「分別」しているのです。そもそも、無理やりに他人の価値を人に押し付けることは人間改造であり、人間を実験動物扱いにしているのに等しいのです。かなり乱暴な言い方をすれば、医療やバイオ・テクノロジーの発展への貢献という「大義」（正義）によって、動物実験者は実験される動物の痛みに気がつかなくなるのと同様に、国家の大望と大義は、それを押し付けられる国民の痛みに気づかないのです。国家ならまだしも、教育に携わる者が、学習者の耐え難き痛みに気づかずにいてそれでよいのでしょうか？

　とは言いましても、現実は自由市場主義が世界を席巻し続けております。いよいよ本格的な「競争」を善とする社会となるようです。歴史の教訓では、戦争が終わり平和が訪れると、戦争景気も終わり、戦争景気に代わる内需拡大に失敗すると戦争が起こると言われております。「万物は流転する」と言いますが、弁証法的に発展すると言われる社会も、まわり戸のように何か中心があって流転するのか、それとも風に散る木の葉のように変幻自在に流転するのか、これも「人知の及ばない」ところです。自由市場主義の競争原理による世界規模での内需拡大が現在の日本の平和の経済的根底でありますが、環境問題とも複雑に絡み合い、これ以上の内需拡大は地球全体の破滅へとつながるようです。ますます複雑になった国際間の利害調節と秩序維持が緊急の課題であり、それにはやはり現在の国際共通語による「コミュニケーション能力」を用いた「国際理解」の理念も不可欠要素の1つとなるようです。

　世界の経済（economics：語源は「共同体のありかた」）の大勢と「国際理解」の成否はさておいて、「共同体（同）化（communicate）」による「共調・同化（assimilation）」は人間改造を前提とした「国際理解」ということなのです。英語教育に携わる多くの人は、この「理解」という概念の狭義の部分に引きずられてか、この趣旨の「国際理解」を標榜しているように思われます。しかしながら本書が提唱する擬似ながらの「国際理解」とは、「対話（talk）」による

「協調（cooperation）」ということです。「対話」とは、いうなれば「人と人とのつきあい」で「ふれあい」であり、哲学者のマルチン・ブーバーは「相手の懸念を、心を開いて受け止め、他人もまたそれを等しく行う行為にほかならない」と定義しています。この「心を開いて受け止める」とは「理解」の達成などは前提にはされておりません。「人と人とのふれあい」や「心を開いて受け止める」ことの前提となるのは「おおらか」な受忍・容認態度であります。したがって、「対話」による「国際理解」には、多少なりともことばによる疎通ができた方が便利かもしれませんが、究極的には、「おおらか」な受忍・容認態度がお互いの心の根底にあれば、それ以上のものはまったく必要ないのです。ですから、世界規模での英語コミュニケーションの強制よりも、文化やことばの障壁を超えた「人と人との心のふれあい」が達成できるほどの「おおらか」な受忍・容認態度に目覚める方が、「国際理解」への貢献度ははるかに大きいし、より人間らしい行為なのです。

　「おおらか」な受忍・容認態度とは一言でいえば、「こだわり」を持たないということです。「こだわり」を持たないとはあまりにもまじめになり過ぎずに「ちょうど"いい加減"」にものごとをとらえるということです。換言すれば、「中庸」の実践であり、究極には「競争の否定」です。人は千差万別であり、その価値観も自ずと違います。それぞれの価値観はそれぞれの主義主張となって表出し、それぞれの行動となります。自分の主義主張は自分なりの正義であり、その正義に「こだわり」を持つのはいいかもしれませんが、しかしながらその正義にあまりにもまじめにこだわり、他人にもその正義を押し付けようとするところから、人と人との紛争は始まるようです。人と人との紛争は「競争」であり、人が他人と競い合うことは他人にこだわることですから、そこに人は自ら自分の自由を失うのです。自らに由って立ち、他者を左右することに固執しない、このような「おおらか」な受忍・容認態度に目覚めた自由人が1人でも多く輩出できるような社会を創造することが「国際理解」に貢献するのではないでしょうか？

　ことばの力を信じ主張する共同体（たとえば英語文化圏）があり、ことばの力に不信を見極め主張しない共同体（たとえば日本語文化圏）もあることをそのまま認め、どちらか一方がもう一方にその価値を無理やりに押し付けずにい

る自由を基調とする世界秩序が「国際理解」へとつながるのではないでしょうか？　ある大国が「理解」に絶対の価値をおき、その国の価値観に照らして適切に「理解」できないものは徹底的に「こだわり」をつけ干渉したり排除したり弾圧する、それに怯える力のない国々はその大国に「理解」されようとやっきになる、このような世界秩序が維持できたとしても、それが日本国憲法に謳う「平和を愛する諸国民の公正と信義に信頼して」成り立つ平和なのでしょうか？

　英語を学習する人あるいは指導する人にとって幸いなことに、英語母語話者の共同体は、自らに由って立ち、他者を左右することに固執しない、このような「おおらか」な受忍・容認態度に目覚めた「国際理解」の実践者の宝庫であります。たとえばアメリカ合州国では、キング牧師やマルコムXなどを挙げることができます。本書第2章ではマルコムXの足跡と彼の残したことば（英語）をとりあげました。「コミュニケーション（会話）」による「生きた英語」ではなく英語で表現された「生きた教え」であります。我々を含め多くの人々に希望と勇気を与える英語です。外国語を学習する真髄は、たとえその外国語を操れなくとも（訓詁学の域を出なくとも）、その外国語を用いて生きる（た）人々の「生きた教え」の生の声（文）に希望を見いだし、感動を受けられることです（この点では、いくらすぐれた翻訳でも自ずと限界があります）。その解説の意味も兼ねて、第3章ではマルコムXの視点から「国際理解教育」を考えてみます。さらに「コミュニケーション能力」とか「語学力」にこだわらず、ただ英語を楽しみたい人のために「暗誦のすすめ」と題して、暗誦の効果的な方法を解説する「手引書」である第4章を設けています。この章で暗誦の手法を身につけられた方は、それを用いて他の章にある英文も楽しんでみられることをぜひお勧めいたします。

第1章　明らめのすすめ

● 明らめのすすめ

　── ものごとは明らめが肝心 ──
と言われます。そして、ひとたび「明らめ」をつけたことには
　── こだわらない ──
ことが賢明である、といわれます。「こだわらない」とは
　── あるがままを受け入れる ──
ということです。

　誤解しないで下さい。「明らめ」は「諦め」ではありません。ここでいう「明らめ」とは「断念」のことではありません。「ものごとを明らかにする」ということです。「ものごと全体の本質をよく見とおす」ということです。

　人間の勝手な分別に基づいた認識や行動とは何かをよくよく明らめる。その明らめによって、理不尽なものごとに執着せず、「こだわり」を捨てる態度が肝要であるということです。

　ですから、ものごとに「黒白をつける」ことが「明らめ」ではないのです。あるいは黒白を比較して、黒が60点で白が40点と判定することではありません。黒は黒で黒の価値があり、白は白で白の価値があり、どちらも100点満点であるとの「こだわり」がない見方をするのが「明らめ」です。

　すなわち、ものごと「一切」からすれば、黒は黒で「一切」と同等の満点の価値を認め、白は白で「一切」と同等の満点の価値を認めるのが「明らめ」です。赤は赤、黄は黄、茶は茶、青は青で、どれもが「一切」と同等の満点の価値なのです。どれもを「あるがまま」に受け入れ「こだわり」を捨てることなのです。

　現代科学においても、「全体は部分の総和でない」ことは改めて確認されてき

たことですが、そのことはとりもなおさず「全体は部分に分けることができない」ことであると認識されつつあります。「森羅万象」と形容される「一切」のものごとの実体は1つ、という見方が科学においても有効になってきたのです。

最も簡明に表現すれば

―― 一切は1つである ――

ということです。「一切は1つ」とは、その「一切」を人間（の心）がどのように分別しても、その分別は「一切」の側から見れば、どれもがかけがえのない存在であり、どれもが平等な価値がある、ということです。

「明らめ」とは、本来はここまで徹底したものなのです。ですから、現実に生身の人間がこのような「明らめ」に到達できるものとはとても思えません。しかしそれでも「諦め」ることはないと思います。「明らめ」に一歩でも歩みを進めるその「歩み」こそが貴重なのです。「明らめ」への人それぞれの「歩み」においてこそ、人は人それぞれの「主体性」を育むことができるからです。

「主体性」とは自由のことです。自由とは

―― 自らを以って由（よし）――

とすることです。ですから、自由とは、自らの「あるがまま」を受け入れることなのです。そうすると必然として他者の「あるがまま」も自己の「あるがまま」のごとく「森羅万象」のなかで、どれもがかけがえのない存在であり、どれもが平等に価値がある、ということが認識できるはずです。

人にとって

―― 明らめとは主体性（自由）の追求 ――

なのです。

「あるがまま」の自分を受け入れられない人、すなわち主体性が奪われた人は、「あるがまま」の他人も受け入れることができません。そのような人は世間や他人の価値観によって支配されてしまっているのです。

そのようにして自由を奪われてしまった心を「奴隷根性」といいます。「奴隷根性」を植え付けられた人は心身ともに奴隷なのです。正真正銘ほんものの奴隷です。ですから、「あるがまま」の自分を受け入れることを追求する「明らめ」とは

―― 自らを奴隷状態から解放する ――

ことにほかならないのです。

● 語学を明らめよう

　さて、本章では、語学、すなわち「外（国）語の習得」を明らめることに、一歩でも近づくことを試みます。無理でも試み自体に意義があることは先ほど述べたとおりです。

　無理があることは明らかです。なぜならば、認知科学や言語学、言語研究の諸分野の研究が急速に発展をとげた現代においてすら、言語や言語習得を体系として説明できる知見を得るにはまだまだ程遠い段階にあるからです。

　裏を返して言えば、人間は言語を使用しているけれども、言語がいったい何なのかを明らめることができていないのです。もしかすると、言語を明らめることは不可能である、と明らめるべきものなのかもしれません。

　特に、「還元主義」による現代の言語学では、人間が勝手に森羅万象と分別した「言語」を記述しようと試みているのみなのです。

　それでもなお、たとえ少しでも言語が明らめられれば、語学を「あるがまま」に受け入れることができるようになります。そうすると多くの人にとって語学が楽しくなってくるに違いありません。

　「努力すれば幸福になる」と考える人が多いように思われます。しかし、これは因果関係を逆にして、「幸福だから努力する」と考えるのも一理あります。楽しいとは幸福なことです。何事も楽しいことには人は夢中になります。寝食すら忘れて何かに夢中に取り組む姿が、他人には「苦を乗り越える努力」と錯覚させてしまうのです。

　話が少しそれましたが、本来、語学は、語学を楽しむことができる人のものです。ですからほんとうに語学を楽しむ人は、自己の語学力については一切「こだわり」がないのです。もちろん、他人の語学力に対しても「こだわり」がありません。

　ですから本来、語学を楽しめない人は語学などやらなくともよいのです。少なくとも、それが自然です。

―― 語学は楽しむもの ――
と明らめて、楽しめない人は語学にこだわらないほうが賢明です。

● 言語と文化とは一体

　新たな言語の獲得とはいかに凄まじいものかを、英語教育学者のダグラス・ブラウン氏は、次のように述べています。

＜外国語習得＞
　Becoming bilingual is a way of life. Your whole person is affected as you struggle to reach beyond the confines of your first language and into a new language, a new culture, a new way of thinking, feeling, and acting. Total commitment, total involvement, a total physical, intellectual, and emotional response is necessary to successfully send and receive message in a second language.
(Brown 1994: 1)

ここでいう
　―― 「total commitment」 ――
これが外国語の獲得なのです。もし本気で母語以外を獲得しようと企てるならば、獲得しようとする言語とその背景である
　―― 「a way of life（＝文化）」 ――
を人間に移植しようとすることなのです。
　多少の誤解をおそれずに表現すれば、人間の主観的自己認識（アイデンティティ）を危機に追いやってしまう完全な狂気なのです。日常のことばで言えば、「自分を自分で自分が誰なのかを分からなくさせてしまう」ということです。
　これは、物質文化の移入や表面的な文化の「ものまね」とはまったく性質の違うものなのです。
　言語と文化とのかかわりを考える背景として、文化について少し概観してみ

ましょう。

　まずは日本文化をみましょう。日本文化の特徴についての言説は膨大な数にのぼりますが、ここでは「total commitment」を考える上で示唆的な言説の1つを紹介します。

　次の英文は本多勝一氏による、日本人の行動原理をおたまじゃくしの行動原理に喩えたものです。ここでいう行動原理（the behavioral principle）とは文化のことです。

＜日本人の行動原理＞

　When I was a child, thousands of tadpoles swam in groups in ponds and rice paddies. On close observation, one would realize that they did not swim in groups because of leadership or from individual will. If one of the group turned sideways, all of them turned sideways. The behavioral principle is to follow what the others are doing.

　The Japanese behavioral principle is like that of tadpoles. Neither theory nor logic nor ethics underlies or informs Japanese behavior. Quite simply, a Japanese looks around and does what others are doing; that is the principle of action. Hence, Japanese have trouble with theory, logic, and ethics; they cannot argue or debate.

　The tadpole society is a product of the Ministry of Education. It is, of course, easy to administer a society of tadpoles. In order to create a tadpole society, the Ministry of Education defines education as regurgitation, and decides what is good to think, while denigrating individual opinion. Individuality is punished, and no one is encouraged to think on one's own. And things are getting worse.

　Perhaps a tadpole society was functional for a village community of the past. But in larger, complex societies, especially in international affairs, it does not work very well.

(Honda 1993: 129-130)

この観察で描写されている「おたまじゃくし型の行動原理」に分類される「regurgitation」とは「total commitment」ではありません。個人の意思や何らかの動機が欠如している上に、当人にとって訳の分からないことを繰り返し復唱するのですから、ここでは「ものまね」と呼んでおきます。個人の自発による動機とは関係のない、主体性の欠如した「ものまね」です。

ちなみに、この「おたまじゃくし型の行動原理」は、「恥の文化」として日本文化をとらえる言説と同様のものです。すなわち、「みんながやっている」「誰もやっていない」ということのみが行動の判断規準となるという一般によく知られている説です。

この「おたまじゃくし型の行動原理」ほどに極端ではありませんが、これによく似た喩えとして、日本文化は「着せ替え人形の文化」だとか「乗り換えの文化」と表現されています。なんでも良いとなる（思い込む）と、急速かつ一斉に古いものを捨てて、新しいものに着替えたり乗り換えたりする、というのです。

日本人の表面上の「一斉の変わり身の早さ」は世界でも有名なようです。近年の「英会話ブーム」もこのこととまったく無関係ではなさそうです。

この「一斉の変わり身の早さ」ゆえに明治以来の急速な日本の「近代化」と、今日の「繁栄」が成し遂げられたと言う人がいますが、確かに大きな要因の1つであることには間違いないでしょう。

日本人はそもそも「何でも比べたがって、どちらが良くてどちらが悪いかということをすぐに決めたがる」、そして「何でも新しいものを良いと決めたがる傾向にある」とよくいわれます（あなた自身にも思い当たるふしはありませんか）。

そして、何かを良いとひとたび決めて（思い込んで）しまうと、猛烈な勢いでそれを追い求めるのに突進してしまう、と観察されているのです。

このような観察の延長線上で、欧米文化、とりわけ第2次大戦後から今日に至るまで、アメリカ文化を「理想の文化」として追い求めることが「日本国家のヴィジョン」の中に仕掛けられた、という極論も多くあります。

進んで選択したのか、嫌でも選択せざるを得なかったのか、何者かに仕掛けられたのかは別として、おおむね日本人の多くは急速にアメリカ文化を「良い」

ものとして追い求め、取り込んだことは間違いない事実と思われます。

もっとも、日本の近代化の特徴としては、西欧化せずに近代化に成功した、と位置付ける見解が大半のようです。近代化の頂点に達しながら、基本となる価値観、生活様式、人間関係、行動規範においては非西欧の精神と体制を維持していると言われています。

日本は近代化を独自の日本文化(もしくは文明)のなかにうまく適応させたのです。

とはいうものの、近代より現代に至るまで「良い」とされる欧米文化の風習や習慣が、少なくとも表面的には極端にまで実現された例として、次の2つの事例を順に考えてみましょう。

＜姓と名の順序＞

Japanese encounter a problem when introducing themselves in English: whether to adapt their names to the English order (with the given name first) or to leave them in the conventional Japanese order (with the surname first). Most ignore the conventions of their own language and place their given names first. The practice, certainly reflecting the Japanese preference, carries over into the media as well. The American press always presents Japanese prime ministers and other newsworthy Japanese with their given names first (while leaving the names of other Asian nationalities in their conventional order). This solution has its merits: when Japanese meet Americans or other foreigners unfamiliar with Japanese name order, they will probably avoid being called Mr.Taro or the like.

The problem posed by name order, however, should not be exaggerated. Many other Asian nationalities who typically place their surnames first in their own language, however, frequently maintain that order in English as well. An individual can easily identify his or her surname when making a self-introduction. And when names appear in context, they generally explain themselves. If a reader, for instance, first reads about Deng Xiaoping and then later about "Deng's reforms," that person instantly understands the conventional order for Chinese names.

More important than the practical matter of daily life, however, are the implications of this convention. When Japanese change their names for the benefit of an American or other foreign listener of western origin, they demonstrate what might be construed as a sense of inferiority toward that person. The corollary of this deferential attitude toward western culture is the sense of superiority demonstrated toward other Asian cultures. When Japanese invert their names, they also attempt to distinguish themselves form other Asians. Why should the name a Japanese person uses in English be any different from that which he or she uses at home? In changing their name order, Japanese make few gains, either in making everyday life more convenient or in establishing a good impression abroad.

(増井他 1992: 32, 34)

英語でも「What's your name?」なんて表現は失礼な言い方です。多くは、「May I have your name?」や「Do you mind If I asked your name?」などと聞かれるように、人にとって名前は非常に大切なものなのです。姓名は生命ともいえるのです。

「名前だけ貸してくれ」なんていう人があなたに近寄ってくれば、その人は「命を貸してくれ」といっているのですから、相当に注意すべきです。

少し話がそれましたが、名前とはその順番も含めて、それほどまでに大切なものなのです。

ところが、大多数の英語の教科書では名前を聞く表現のあとに「My name is Ichiro Suzuki.」のように、本来の姓と名の順番を逆転させて、対話練習させようとします。そのせいか、多くの日本人がこの習慣を身につけてしまうようです。

最近では、少しずつこの奇妙さに気づいてか、「I am Suzuki Ichiro.」のようにする人も多くいます。

また、第22期国語審議会（平成12年）でも、日本人の姓名のローマ字表記に関し、「姓-名」の順とすることが望ましいとし、官公庁や報道機関等におけ

る表記および学校教育における英語などの指導において、その趣旨が生かされることを希望しています。

いくら「アメリカ文化」を理想とする人もやはり名前は主観的自己認識（アイデンティティ）と深いかかわりがあるからでしょうか、日本語で自分の名前を述べるときにまで、逆転させる人はめったにいないようです。

しかし、次の事例はいかがでしょう。先ほどの「おたまじゃくしの喩え」の著者である本多勝一氏が日本国内で、しかも日本人どうしでの体験を語ったものです。

＜植民地根性＞

Last summer, I went with a friend to a restaurant in a large Tokyo hotel. The evening view overlooking the Imperial Palace was especially beautiful. However, we could not enter the restaurant because we were not dressed appropriately. It was unfortunate, but nothing could be done.

I suppose that in countries like England and France, to which we aspire in our modernization efforts, dress codes are if anything more strict. I asked: "Then what should we wear?" The reply: "At least a coat. However, women can wear anything" "What if we wore traditional Japanese clothing?" The man at the counter paused and then answered: "No, you must wear Western clothes." "What if some Arab come in wearing Arabic clothing?" He paused again and said maliciously: "Well, it depends on the situation but I cannot decide, so perhaps you should ask the manager."

We can see the "colonized" spirit of Japanese hotels. They do not recognize traditional Japanese clothing — what we wear to weddings — as appropriate. If I wore traditional clothes, whether Japanese or Arab, to a first-rate hotel in Paris or London, I would assume that it would be appropriate.

I once went to a hotel in Hanoi that had been constructed during the French colonial period. I felt as though I had come to the Paris of the Bourbon monarchy. However, in the main restaurant of the hotel, the waitresses didn't speak any language other than Vietnamese. They were very kind and friendly, but they didn't find it necessary to know other languages. In contrast, at a first-class restaurant in Saigon (then South Vietnam), there are many waitresses and waiters who speak French or English. When I try to speak in Vietnamese, they look at me scornfully as someone who can't speak French or English. This is the spirit of the colonized; I am afraid that the Japanese are becoming like that.

(Honda 1993: 138-139)

　レストラン側の気持ちもよく分かります。ここでも言っているとおり、場所と機会に適切な服装（dress codes）というものがありますし、西欧風の高級レストランとしての「ふさわしい雰囲気」を保つ必要と責務があるのは当然でしょう。
　しかしながら「ふさわしい雰囲気」を作り上げるのは社会の風潮でもあります。その許容範囲に日本の正装を排すべきとまで考えさせることは、とりもなおさず「日本のものはすべて良くない」と思う人が、そのレストランの客の大半を占める（とレストランが考えている）からです。（最近ではこのような極端な傾向は変化してきたと思われます。）
　程度の差こそあれ、このような風潮を「拝外主義」といいます。その反対に、自文化のもの意外であれば「良し」としないことを「排外主義」といいます。
　拝外主義、排外主義のいずれであっても、やはり極端に走るのはいかなものでしょうか。先に見た日本文化の「おたまじゃくし型の行動原理」や「着せ替え人形の文化」は、日本人が自己を知る1つの示唆としてとらえておくのがよいでしょう。
　ここで以上の文化の概観が「言語」にどのような示唆を与えるのかを考えてみましょう。
　着物や飾りなどであれば、身の外に着けるだけで済みます。さて、外国語学習、すなわち異文化の言語である母語以外の言語の場合はどこにまとおうとしているのでしょうか。
　もちろん、母語と同じく心身、すなわち人間そのものに言語を一体化させようとしているのです。

人間を心と身体に分けるのは、人間の勝手な分別に基づくものです。同様に、言語と人間を分けるのも、人間の勝手な分別に基づくものなのです。このことは、「人間なしでは言語が存在し得ない」ということを少し考えただけでもすぐに認識できるはずです。
　この点が物質文化の移入や表層文化の移入と外（国）語の獲得との大きな違いなのです。
　着物や飾りでさえも、一見それを身に装う人に何の影響も与えないように思われがちですが、着物や飾りが中身を作り上げることはよく知られています。（ですから、身だしなみも大切なこととされるのです。）それでもあくまで着物や飾りはあくまでも身の外にまとうだけです。
　しかしながら、
　── 言語と人間は一体 ──
ではありませんか。
　もちろん、「言語と人間は一体」というとらえ方だけで言語の特質のすべてを説明できません。それでもなお、言語は「ただの道具」と位置づけてしまえば、言語と人間のかかわりの深さを、あまりにも矮小化した見方になってしまいます。
　この意味において、言語は人間そのものなのですから、
　── 言語は人間の主体性 ──
と深くかかわりがあると言えるのです。
　ここで、「人間の行動原理」としての文化について簡潔かつ的確な記述がありますので、熟読してみましょう。本節冒頭で紹介した、外国語習得を「total commitment」としてとらえる立場の英語教育学者ダグラス・ブラウン氏によるものです。

<文化>

　Culture is a way of life. Culture is the context within which we exist, think, and relate to others. It is the "glue" that binds a group of people together.

<中略>

　Culture might be defined as the ideas, customs, skills, arts, tools, and so forth that characterize a given group of people in a given period of time. But culture is more than the sum of its parts. It is a system of integrated patterns, most of which remain below the threshold of consciousness, yet all of which govern human behavior just as surely as the manipulated strings of a puppet control its motions. The fact that no society exists without a culture reflects the need for culture to fulfill certain biological and psychological needs in human being. Consider the bewildering host of confusing and contradictory facts and propositions and ideas that present themselves every day to any human being; some organization of these facts is necessary to provide some order to potential chaos, and therefore, conceptual networks of reality evolve within a group of people for such organization. The mental constructs that enable us to survive are a way of life that we call "culture."

(Brown 1994: 163-164)

　文化とは
　―「a way of life」―
であり、
　―「conceptual networks of reality」―
であると述べています。
　ここでいう「conceptual networks of reality」は、人間が身につける個別の言語に深く関連するものです。そうすると、言語は「a way of life」の拠り所の1つでもあることになります。
　この意味において、言語と文化は密接な関係にあり、相互に影響を及ぼし合っているのです。端的に言えば

―― 言語と文化は一体 ――
なのです。
　たとえ言語が文化の部分というとらえ方を採用しても、文化は「more than the sum of its parts」(すなわちゲシュタルト) なのですから、全体としては文化と言語とを分別することは不可能なのです。
　ですから、言語は「行動原理」と切り離すことはできないのです。
　このような状態を別名では「ことばの牢獄」と言います。「ことばの牢獄」は、終身そこから出ることができません。
　そうすると、外 (国) 語の獲得は、とりもなおさず別の新たな「conceptual networks of reality」の獲得となり、別の新たな「a way of life」の獲得ということになります。新たな別の「行動原理」の獲得ということにもつながります。
　これでお分かりいただけたと思いますが、もし本気で母語以外を獲得しようと企てるならば、既存の「conceptual networks of reality」と「a way of life」である母語体系をそのままに、獲得しようとする言語体系の「conceptual networks of reality」と「a way of life」を自身に植えつけることなのです。
　これは、物質文化の移入や表層文化 (名前の場合はことばの本質的なものを含むので少し違う) の「おたまじゃくし型の行動原理」のような主体性が欠如した「ものまね」とはまったく性質の違う
　―― 「total commitment」 ――
なのです。

● 「total commitment」は狂気

　ここまででお分かりいただけると思いますが、外 (国) 語の獲得のみが語学ならば、語学は「total commitment」でしかありません。
　しかしながら、いきなり「total commitment」を追い求めても無理があり過ぎます。それに外 (国) 語の「獲得」のみを語学の目的にしなければならない、という制約はありません。考えようによっては、狂っています。
　次の英文は、歴史上の事実のなかで「total commitment」が政治によって強

制された「狂気」を物語るものです。

Language − Life of a People

　Do you know anything about Wales? It is in the west of Great Britain. The people there love singing. The song they love the best is "Land of My Fathers". It is a song about their history and their language.
　When some pubs close at night, people begin to sing "Land of My Fathers". They never forget their unhappy history.
　Before 1536 Wales was an independent country. People in Wales spoke their own Language, Welsh. But Wales was conquered by England, and in 1536 through the Act of Union it became a part of England.
　The law made English the official language in Wales.
　After 1870 children had to use English at school. If they spoke any Welsh, they had to wear a piece of wood round their neck. The piece of wood said "Welsh Not". These children were punished when school was over.
　Similar tragedies happened in other countries too. Korea is one of them.
　Korea was a colony of Japan for thirty-five years. The Japanese government forced the Koreans to use only Japanese. It was really painful for them to stop using their own language. They could not use it again in public until the end of World War II.
　Today there are about 2,900,000 people in Wales. Only 19 percent of them are able to speak Welsh. All the rest speak only English. Some people say that Welsh will die out in the 21st century. They are really sorry about that. So schools now have Welsh classes to keep the language alive.
　Language is the life of the people who use it.
　　　　　　　　　　(*New Crown English Series* New Edition 3　1997：80-83)

　人間は、言語、宗教、歴史、祖先、価値観、生活習慣、社会制度などによって自分を定義するものである、と言われています。自分たちはいったい誰なの

かという問いに答えられることが、人間が直面する最も基本的な問いなのです。これが、主観的自己認識（アイデンティティ）と呼ばれるものです。

　裏を返して言うならば、個々人の意識が、日本人なら日本人（共同体）、アメリカ人ならアメリカ人（共同体）という観念を作り上げているのです。

　言語も同じです。個々人の意識が、日本語なら日本語、英語なら英語という観念を作り上げているのです。言語の違いとはそのようなものです。お互いどうしが通じ合うとか通じ合わないとかいうのは、言語と言語を分ける絶対の規準ではありません。

　たとえば、スペイン語とポルトガル語はかなりの程度通じますが、別々の言語です。その反対に、中国語のようにお互いに理解できない方言がかなりあるにもかかわらず、1つの言語という意識があります。

　ですから、この意味において
── 言語は主観的自己認識とのかかわりが深い ──
とよく言われるのです。

　したがって、お互い通じ合う言語どうしであろうとも、お互い理解できない言語どうしであろうとも、ある人が母語でない言語を用いようとすると、その人の主観的自己認識（アイデンティティ）を大きく揺るがすことになるのです。

　試しに、あなたの日常のことばとは違う方言で、しばらく日本語を話してみて下さい。どんな気持ちがしますか？

　たとえば、もしもあなたが関西人であるとして東京の方言を用いることを無理やり強制され、できなかったらといって罰を受けたと想像してみて下さい。それって、まぎれもなく「いじめ」ですよね？

　歴史の上では、権力と言語とは常に深いかかわりがありました。簡単に言うと、弱いものいじめです。

<権力と言語>

　Throughout history the distribution of languages in the world has reflected the distribution of power in the world. The most widely spoken languages ── English, Mandarin, Spanish, French, Arabic, Russian ── are or were the languages of imperial states which actively promoted use of their languages by other peoples. Shifts in the distribution of power produce shifts in the use of languages. .... Britain and French insisted on the use of their languages in their colonies. Following independence, however, most of the former colonies attempted in varying degrees and with varying success to replace the imperial language with indigenous ones. During the heyday of the Soviet Union, Russian was the lingua franca from Prague to Hanoi. The decline of Russian power is accompanied by a parallel decline in the use of Russian as a second language. As with other forms of culture, increasing power generates both linguistic assertiveness by native speakers and incentives to learn the language by others. In the heady days immediately after the Berlin Wall came down and it seemed as if the united Germany was the new behemoth, there was a noticeable tendency for Germans fluent in English to speak German at international meetings. Japanese economic power has stimulated the learning of Japanese by non-Japanese, and the economic development of China is producing a similar boom in Chinese. Chinese is rapidly displacing English as the predominant language in Hong Kong and, given the role of the overseas Chinese in Southeast Asia, has become the language in which much of that area's international business is transacted. As the power of the West gradually declines relative to that of other civilizations, the use of English and other Western languages in other societies and for communications between societies will also slowly erode. If at some point in the distant future China displaces the West as the dominant civilization in the world, English will give way to Mandarin as the world's lingua franca.

(Huntington 1996: 62-63)

　これでお分かりのように、現在の全地球（global）の権力（power）の構造こそが、我々日本語を母語とする日本人に「伝達（コミュニケーション）の手段としての英語」を身につけさせようと仕向けているのです。
　お気づきかと思います。「伝達（コミュニケーション）の手段としての英語」とはまさに「total commitment」としての語学ではありませんか？

権力が行う言語の支配（control）を言語政策と呼びます。「total commitment」としての語学を社会全体の規模で政治の力で行う言語政策を、言語の「同化政策」と呼びます。

　政策の判断のよしあし、社会全体の利益は別の問題として、言語の同化政策が「total commitment」としての語学の強制であるとき、それは個人の主観的自己認識（アイデンティティ）を根底から破壊する狂気となるのです。

● ここは日本、日本語でしゃべれ

　狂気の語学が、日本で行われていることを証明するかのように近年では
── 日本では、日本語でしゃべれ ──
という当然の主張をする人も多くなったようです。

　当然のことならば本当は主張しなくともよいのですが、敢えて主張しなければならないところに、日本における語学、とりわけ英語に対する大多数の日本人の意識の異常さを物語っています。

　この現状を狂気ととらえる論客の1人である津田幸男氏は「英語支配からの解放を目指す新たな意識確立のための21の提言」を提唱しています。我々日本人の英語に対する意識を考える上でおおいに参考になりますので紹介しておきましょう。

A　英語に関して
  1. 英語は数千もある世界中の言語の1つにすぎないと認識すること。
  2. 英語は世界支配語であり、弱者抑圧語であると認識すること。
  3. 現在少数の英語民族が多数の非英語民族を支配していることを認識すること。
  4. 英語に付け加えられた「先進」「進歩」「優秀」といった差別的な付加価値を否定すること。
  5. 英語が話せないことは恥ではなく、逆に話せることは偉いことではないと認識すること。

6. 英語学習は個人の主体的欲求から行われるべきで、その欲求は社会的なプロパガンダによりかきたてられたものであってはいけない。

B　ガイジン（つまり欧米人）に関して
7. 日本国内でガイジンには英語で話す必要はないと認識すること。
8. 何年日本にいても、日本語を話そうとしない外人は、日本人への敬意がないと認識すること。
9. ガイジンに媚びることも、排他することもなく、対等な人間として対応すること。
10. ガイジンに付けられた「先進」「進歩」「優秀」といった差別的な付加価値は誤りであると認識すること。
11. 日本はガイジンを優遇し、非西洋諸国の外国人を冷遇する差別的社会であることを認識すること。

（津田は「ガイジン」という用語を、日本人の多くが欧米白人を指して使う際の呼称として用いている）

C　日本人の自我に関して
12. 日本人としての肯定的な自画像を確立すること。
13. 西洋との関係における日本人の自我の葛藤を認識すること。
14. 日本人の自我の中の「抑圧」を知り、その歴史的ルーツと、底に潜む支配関係を認識すること。
15. 西洋的自我の模倣でなく、日本人が主体的に欲求する自我の追及を正直に行うべきである。
16. 日本人の統一的な自我には日本語が不可欠であることを認識すること。

D　国際化に関して
17. 英語が話せることと、国際人とは無関係であると認識すること。
18. 日本人の意識の国際化が必要であり、それは英会話では達成できないと認識すること。
19. 意識の国際化とは究極的には人間、言語、文化の徹底した平等を遵守する態度と認識すること。

20. 西洋化と国際化を混同すべきではない。西洋化とは模倣だが、国際化とは古い意識の破壊と新たな意識の創造を指すと認識すること。
21. 国際人とは無国籍人間ではなく、日本人としての肯定的な自画像を持つ人であると認識すること。

（津田 1990: 196-8、1993: 48-54）

　いかがでしょうか？　津田氏の提言に多少の意見の相違があったとしても、おおむね
　── 日本では、日本語でしゃべれ ──
という主張は、当然のものだと思われませんか？
　少なくとも、あなたの母語が否定されない、というのは、
　── あるがままをあるがまま受け入れよ ──
ということではないでしょうか。

● 世界人権宣言

　ものごとを明らめるとは、
　── あるがままをあるがまま受け入れる ──
ということです。
　ところが、ものごとを明らめるのは、非常に難しいものです。あるがままがあるがままとして、なかなか見定められないのです。
　特に、善悪に関するあるがままを断定することは不可能です。唯一、善悪を決める役割を担えるのは宗教です。ですから宗教が、個々人の主観的自己認識（アイデンティティ）や文化の中核の1つとしてとらえられるのが、あるがままの姿なのです。でなければ、そうあるべきものなのです。
　ともあれ、それぞれの社会で当然と判定されたことが、その社会での「あたりまえ」となります。
　「あたりまえ」とされたものは、当然私たちが主張できる事柄です。法の支配による近代社会では「権利」として表現されているものが、「あたりまえ」の

1つの規準と言えるでしょう。
　権利の中でも特に、「人権」は、人間としての「あたりまえ」を判定したものです。その集大成の1つとして有名なものが「世界人権宣言」ですので、ここで紹介いたします。
　社会の取り決め（法律や規範など）は、先ほどの文化についての記述における「conceptual networks of reality」の1つです。ですから1つの「フィクション」です。その意味においてこの「世界人権宣言」も「フィクション」なのです。そこから「a way of life」、すなわちものの見方や考え方をよく観察する価値があるものです。（人権についての国際的な取り決めとしては「国際人権規約（西暦1996年に国連総会が採択）」のほうがより微細です。）
　「世界人権宣言」は西暦1948年12月10日に国連総会で採択されたものです。アメリカを中心とする「国際化」という制約のなかで国際連合が発足（西暦1945年10月24日）したおよそ3年後のことです。（一般に国際社会のなかでアメリカ的価値と言われるものが「人権」と「民主主義」と「市場経済」との3つです。）
　「世界人権宣言」は各社会それぞれの「あたりまえ」を超えて、「あるがまま」を志しているように思われます。一見そのように見えるだけかもしれません。そのあたりの吟味は、読者それぞれにお任せします。
　この「世界人権宣言」という枠組みの中でも、言語に関する「あたりまえ」が主張されています。その直接の部分は第2条なのですが、宣言全体での文脈で第2条をとらえた方がより奥深い意味が味わえますので、宣言すべてをぜひ詳細にお読み下さい。ここでも、部分と全体は不可分なのだと心得て下さい。
　そうすると、「total commitment」としての語学を政治の力で強制することは、いかに人が人を抑圧することなのかが明らかになるでしょう。「total commitment」としての語学を推進するような社会制度を政策として巧みに仕組むのも同等です。
　なお、英語学習者にとって「世界人権宣言」は、第4章で紹介するような方法で暗誦するのに最適なものの1つと著者が信じるものです。多くの国連職員が（なぜか英語で）暗誦したり、いつもカバンの中に入れて持ち歩いているので有名なものの1つです。条文なので表現が少々形式ばっていますが、そのぶ

ん内容が厳密なので「暗誦」しやすいものです。条文ごとに少しずつ進めれば、無理なく「暗誦」できます。

＜世界人権宣言＞

THE UNIVERSAL DECLARATION OF HUMAN RIGHTS

ADOPTED BY THE UNITED NATIONS GENERAL ASSEMBLY
10 DECEMBER, 1948

WHEREAS recognition of the inherent dignity and of the equal and inalienable rights of all members of the human family is the foundation of freedom, justice and peace in the world,

WHEREAS disregard and contempt for human rights have resulted in barbarous acts which have outraged the conscience of mankind, and the advent of a world in which human beings shall enjoy freedom of speech and belief and freedom from fear and want has been proclaimed as the highest aspiration of the common people,

WHEREAS it is essential, if man is not to be compelled to have recourse, as a last resort, to rebellion against tyranny and oppression, that human rights should be protected by the rule of law,

WHEREAS it is essential to promote the development of friendly relations between nations,

WHEREAS the peoples of the United Nations have in the Charter reaffirmed their faith in fundamental human rights, in the dignity and worth of the human person and in the equal rights of men and women and have determined to promote social progress and better standards of life in larger freedom,

WHEREAS Member States have pledged themselves to achieve, in cooperation with the United Nations, the promotion of universal respect for and observance of human rights and fundamental freedoms,

WHEREAS a common understanding of these rights and freedoms is of the greatest importance for the full realisation of this pledge,

Now, therefore, THE GENERAL ASSEMBLY proclaims this Universal Declaration of Human Rights as a common standard of achievement for all peoples and all nations, to the end that every individual and every organ of society, keeping this Declaration constantly in mind, shall strive by teaching and education to promote respect for these rights and freedoms and by progressive measures, national and international, to secure their universal and effective recognition and observance, both among the peoples of the Member States themselves and among the peoples of territories under their jurisdiction.

ARTICLE 1. All human beings are born free and equal in dignity and rights. They are endowed with reason and conscience and should act towards one another in a spirit of brotherhood.

ARTICLE 2. (1) Everyone is entitled to all the rights and freedoms set forth in this Declaration, without distinction of any kind, such as race, colour, sex, language, religion, political or other opinion, national or social origin, property, birth or other status.

(2) Furthermore, no distinction shall be made on the basis of the political, jurisdictional or international status of the country or territory to which a person belongs, whether it be independent, trust, non-self-governing or under any other limitation of sovereignty.

ARTICLE 3. Everyone has the right to life, liberty and security of person.

ARTICLE 4. No one shall be held in slavery or servitude; slavery and the slave trade shall be prohibited in all their forms.

ARTICLE 5. No one shall be subjected to torture or to cruel, inhuman or degrading treatment or punishment.

ARTICLE 6. Everyone has the right to recognition everywhere as a person before the law.

ARTICLE 7. All are equal before the law and are entitled without any discrimination to equal protection of the law. All are entitled to equal protection against any discrimination in violation of this Declaration and against any incitement to such discrimination.

ARTICLE 8. Everyone has the right to an effective remedy by the competent national tribunals for acts violating the fundamental rights granted him by the constitution or by law.

ARTICLE 9. No one shall be subjected to arbitrary arrest, detention or exile.

ARTICLE 10. Everyone is entitled in full equality to a fair and public hearing by an independent and impartial tribunal, in the determination of his rights and obligations and of any criminal charge against him.

ARTICLE 11. (1) Everyone charged with a penal offence has the right to be presumed innocent until proved guilty according to law in a public trial at which he has had all the guarantees necessary for his defence.

(2) No one shall be held guilty of any penal offence on account of any act or omission which did not constitute a penal offence, under national or international law, at the time when it was committed. Nor shall a heavier penalty be imposed than the one that was applicable at the time the penal offence was committed.

ARTICLE 12. No one shall be subjected to arbitrary interference with his privacy, family, home or correspondence, nor to attacks upon his honour and reputation. Everyone has the right to the protection of the law against such interference or attacks.

ARTICLE 13. (1) Everyone has the right to freedom of movement and residence within the borders of each State.

(2) Everyone has the right to leave any country, including his own, and to return to his country.

ARTICLE 14. (1) Everyone has the right to seek and to enjoy in other countries asylum from persecution.

(2) This right may not be invoked in the case of prosecutions genuinely arising form non-political crimes or from acts contrary to the purposes and principles of the United Nations.

ARTICLE 15. (1) Everyone has the right to a nationality.

(2) No one shall be arbitrarily deprived of his nationality nor denied the right to change his nationality.

ARTICLE 16. (1) Men and women of full age, without any limitation due to race, nationality or religion, have the right to marry and to found a family. They are entitled to equal rights as to marriage, during marriage and at its dissolution.

(2) Marriage shall be entered into only with the free and full consent of the intending spouses.

(3) The family is the natural and fundamental group unit of society and is entitled to protection by society and the State.

ARTICLE 17. (1) Everyone has the right to own property alone as well as in association with others.

(2) No one shall be arbitrarily deprived of his property.

ARTICLE 18. Everyone has the right to freedom of thought, conscience and religion; this right includes freedom to change his religion or belief, and freedom, either alone or in community with others and in public or private, to manifest his religion or belief in teaching, practice, worship and observance.

ARTICLE 19. Everyone has the right to freedom of opinion and expression; this right includes freedom to hold opinions without interference and to seek, receive and impart information and ideas through any media and regardless of frontiers.

ARTICLE 20. (1) Everyone has the right to freedom of peaceful assembly and association.

(2) No one may be compelled to belong to an association.

ARTICLE 21. (1) Everyone has the right to take part in the government of his country, directly or through chosen representatives.

(2) Everyone has the right of equal access to public service in his country.

(3) The will of the people shall be the basis of the authority of government; this will shall be expressed in periodic and genuine elections which shall be held by universal and equal suffrage and shall be held by secret vote or by equivalent free voting procedures.

ARTICLE 22. Everyone, as a member of society, has the right to social security and is entitled to realisation, through national effort and international cooperation and in accordance with the organisation and resources of each State, of the economic, social and cultural rights indispensable for his dignity and the free development of his personality.

ARTICLE 23. (1) Everyone has the right to work, to free choice of employment, to just and favourable conditions of work and to protection against unemployment.

(2) Everyone, without any discrimination, has the right to equal pay for equal work.

(3) Everyone has the right to just and favourable remuneration ensuring for himself and his family an existence worthy of human dignity, and supplemented, if necessary, by other means of social protection.

(4) Everyone has the right to form and to join trade unions for the protection of his interests.

ARTICLE 24. Everyone has the right to rest and leisure, including reasonable limitation of working hours and periodic holidays with pay.

ARTICLE 25. (1) Everyone has the right to a standard of living adequate for the health and well-being of himself and of his family, including food, clothing, housing and medical care and necessary social services, and the right to security in the event of unemployment, sickness, disability, widowhood, old age and other lack of livelihood in circumstances beyond his control.

(2) Motherhood and childhood are entitled to special care and assistance.

All children, whether born in or out of wedlock, shall enjoy the same social protection.

ARTICLE 26. (1) Everyone has the right to education. Education shall be free, at least in the elementary and fundamental stages. Elementary education shall be compulsory. Technical and professional education shall be made generally available and higher education shall be equally accessible to all on the basis of merit.

(2) Education shall be directed to the full development of the human personality and to the strengthening of respect for human rights and fundamental freedoms. It shall promote understanding, tolerance and friendship among all nations, racial or religious groups, and shall further the activities of the United Nations for the maintenance of peace.

(3) Parents have a prior right to choose the kind of education that shall be given their children.

ARTICLE 27. (1) Everyone has the right to freely participate in the cultural life of the community, to enjoy the arts and to share in scientific advancement and its benefits.

(2) Everyone has the right to the protection of the moral and material interests resulting from any scientific, literary or artistic production of which he is the author.

ARTICLE 28. Everyone is entitled to a social and international order in which the rights and freedoms set forth in this Declaration can be fully realised.

ARTICLE 29. (1) Everyone has duties to the community in which alone the free and full development of his personality is possible.

(2) In the exercise of his rights and freedoms, everyone shall be subject only to such limitations as are determined by law solely for the purpose of securing due recognition and respect for the rights and freedoms of others and of meeting the just requirements of morality, public order and the general welfare in a democratic society.

(3) These rights and freedoms may in no case be exercised contrary to the purposes and principles of the United Nations.

ARTICLE 30. Nothing in this Declaration may be interpreted as implying for any State, group or person any right to engage in any activity or to perform any act aimed at the destruction of any of the rights and freedoms set forth herein.

以上＜世界人権宣言＞

● 世界言語権宣言

「total commitment」としての語学を強制される人の痛みがいかに激しいものかは、人間社会はまだまだ充分に認識していないようです。抑圧されている本人ですら、まったく認識していないこともありますから、非常にたちの悪いものです。

そのような状況のなかで近年、

── 言語権 ──

という考え方がしだいに輪郭を現してきました。言語についての「あるがまま」を見定めようとする営みの1つです。

その言語権という考え方の1つの先駆けとして位置付けられるものが、次に全文を紹介したい「世界言語権宣言」です。ぜひ詳細に熟読されることを推薦いたします。

「世界言語権宣言」は、西暦1996年6月にスペインのバルセロナにて開催された世界言語権会議で採択されたものです。この会議は国際ペンクラブの翻訳・言語権委員会ならびにＣＩＥＭＥＮ（少数民族の調査・研究・支援を行う非政府組織）の呼びかけたもので、90か国から220人（66団体のＮＧＯ、41のペンセンター、41人の言語法制の専門家など）の参加によって開催されたものです。

「世界言語権宣言」は現段階ではまだ非政府レベルのイニシアティブですが、その内容は、これまでの言語に関する人間の知見のすべてが集約されています。

ですから、「世界言語権宣言」はそのままで言語学の精要であり、現代言語学の絶好の基本書としても利用できます。

＜世界言語権宣言＞

UNIVERSAL DECLARATION ON LINGUISTIC RIGHTS

PRELIMINARIES

The institutions and non-governmental organizations, signatories to the present Universal Declaration of Linguistic Rights, meeting in Barcelona from 6 to 9 June 1996,

Having regard to the 1948 Universal Declaration of Human Rights which, in its preamble, expresses its "faith in fundamental human rights, in the dignity and worth of the human person and in the equal rights of men and women"; and which, in its second article, establishes that "everyone is entitled to all the rights and freedoms" regardless of "race, colour, sex, language, religion, political or other opinion, national or social origin, property, birth or other status";

Having regard to the International Covenant on Civil and Political Rights of 16 December 1966 (Article 27), and the International Covenant on Economic, Social and Cultural Rights of the same date which, in their preambles, state that human beings cannot be free unless conditions are created which enable them to enjoy both their civil and political rights and their economic, social and cultural rights;

Having regard to Resolution 47/135 of 18 December 1992 of the General Assembly of the United Nations Organizations which adopted the Declaration on the Rights of Persons belonging to National, Ethnic, Religious and Linguistic Minorities;

Having regard to the declarations and conventions of the Council of Europe, such as the European Convention for the Protection of Human Rights and Fundamental Freedoms, of 4 November 1950 (Article 14); the Convention of the Council of Ministers of the Council of Europe, of 29 June 1992, approving the European Charter for Regional or Minority Languages; the Declaration on National Minorities by the Summit Meeting of the Council of Europe on 9 October 1993; and the Framework Convention for the Protection of National Minorities of November 1994;

Having regard to the Santiago de Compostela Declaration of the International PEN Club and the Declaration of 15 December 1993 of the Translations and Linguistic Rights Committee of the International PEN Club concerning the proposal to hold a World Conference on Linguistic Rights;

Considering that, in the Recife, Brazil, Declaration of 9 October 1987, the 12th Seminar of the International Association for the Development of Intercultural Communication recommended the United Nations Organization to take the necessary steps to approve and implement a Universal Declaration on Linguistic Rights;

Having regard to Convention 169 of the International Labour Organization of 26 June 1989 concerning Indigenous and Tribal Peoples in Independent Countries;

Having regard to the Universal Declaration of the Collective Rights of Peoples, Barcelona, May 1990, which declared that all peoples have the right to express and develop their culture, language and rules of organization and, to this end, to adopt political, educational, communications and governmental structures of their own, within different political frameworks;

Having regard to the Final Declaration of the General Assembly of the International Federation of Modern Language Teachers in Pécs (Hungary) on 16 August 1991, which recommended that linguistic rights be considered among the fundamental rights of the individual;

Having regard to the report of the Human Rights Commission of the United Nations Economic and Social Council, of 20 April 1994, concerning the draft Declaration on the Rights of Indigenous Peoples, which assesses individual rights in the light of collective rights;

Having Regard to the draft Declaration of the Inter-American Human Rights Commission on the Rights of Indigenous Peoples, approved at session 1278 on 18 September 1995;

Considering that the majority of the world's endangered languages belong to non-sovereign peoples and that the main factors which prevent the development of these languages and accelerate the process of language substitution include the lack of self-government and the policy of states which impose their political and administrative structures and their language;

Considering that invasion, colonization, occupation and other instances of political, economic or social subordination often involve the direct imposition of a foreign language or, at the very least, distort perceptions of the value of languages and give rise to hierarchical linguistic attitudes which undermine the language loyalty of speakers; and considering that the languages of some peoples which have attained sovereignty are immersed in a process of language substitution as a result of a policy which favours the language of a former colonial or imperial power;

Considering that universalism must be based on a conception of linguistic and cultural diversity which prevails over trends towards homogenization and exclusionary isolation;

Considering that, in order to ensure peaceful coexistence between language communities, a series of overall principles must be found so as to guarantee the promotion and respect of all languages and their social use in public and in private;

Considering that various factors of an extralinguistic nature (historical, political, territorial, demographic, economic, sociocultural and sociolinguistic factors and those related to collective attitudes) give rise to problems which lead to the extinction, marginalization and degeneration of numerous languages, and that consequently linguistic rights must be examined in an overall perspective, so as to apply appropriate solutions in each case;

In the belief that a Universal Declaration of Linguistic Rights is required in order to correct linguistic imbalances with a view to ensuring the respect and full development of all languages and establishing the principles for a just and equitable linguistic peace throughout the world as a key factor in the maintenance of harmonious social relations;

HEREBY DECLARE THAT

PREAMBLE

The situation of each language, in view of the foregoing considerations, is the result of the convergence and interaction of a wide range of factors of a political and legal, ideological and historical, demographic and territorial, economic and social, cultural, linguistic and sociolinguistic, interlinguistic and subjective nature.

More specifically, at the present time, these factors are defined by:

. The age-old unifying tendency of the majority of states to reduce diversity and foster attitudes opposed to cultural plurality and linguistic pluralism.

. The trend towards a worldwide economy and consequently towards a worldwide market of information, communications and culture, which disrupts the spheres of interrelation and the forms of interaction that guarantee the internal cohesion of language communities.

. The economicist growth model put forward by transnational economic groups which seeks to identify deregulation with progress and competitive individualism with freedom and generates serious and growing economic, social, cultural and linguistic inequality.

Language communities are currently under pressure from dangers arising from a lack of self-government, a limited population or one that is partially or wholly dispersed, a fragile economy, an uncodified language, or a cultural model opposed to the dominant one, which make it impossible for many languages to survive and develop unless the following basic goals are taken into account:

. In a political perspective, the goal of conceiving a way of organizing linguistic diversity so as to permit the effective participation of language communities in this new growth model.

. In a cultural perspective, the goal of rendering the worldwide communications space compatible with the equitable participation of all peoples, language communities and individuals in the development process.

. In an economic perspective, the goal of fostering sustainable development based on the participation of all and on respect for the ecological balance of societies and for equitable relationships between all languages and cultures.

For all these reasons, this Declaration takes language communities and not states as its point of departure and is to be viewed in the context of the reinforcement of international institutions capable of guaranteeing sustainable and equitable development for the whole of humanity. For these reasons also it aims to encourage the creation of a political framework for linguistic diversity based upon respect, harmonious coexistence and mutual benefit.

PRELIMINARY TITLE
Concepts

Article 1
1. This Declaration considers as a language community any human society established historically in a particular territorial space, whether this space be recognized or not, which identifies itself as a people and has developed a common language as a natural means of communication and cultural cohesion between its members. The term language specific to a terrritory refers to the language of the community historically established in such a space.

2. This Declaration takes as its point of departure the principle that linguistic rights are individual and collective at one and the same time. In defining the full range of linguistic rights, it adopts as its referent the case of a historical

language community within its own territorial space, this space being understood, not only as the geographical area where the community lives, but also as the social and functional space vital to the full development of the language. Only on this basis is it possible to define the rights of the language groups mentioned in point 5 of the present article, and those of individuals living outside the territory of their community, in terms of a gradation or continuum.

3. For the purpose of this Declaration, groups are also deemed to be in their own territory and to belong to a language community in the following circumstances:
i. when they are separated from the main body of their community by political or administrative boundaries;
ii. when they have been historically established in a small area surrounded by members of otherlanguage communities; or
iii. when they are established in an area which they share with the members of other language communities with similar historical antecedents.

4. This Declaration also considers nomad peoples within their historical areas of migration and peoples historically established in geographically dispersed locations as language communities in their own territory.

5. This Declaration considers as a language group any group of persons sharing the same language which is established in the territorial space of another language community but which does not possess historical antecedents equivalent to those of that community. Examples of such groups are immigrants, refugees, deported persons and members of diasporas.

Article 2
1. This Declaration considers that, whenever various language communities

and groups share the same territory, the rights formulated in this Declaration must be exercised on a basis of mutual respect and in such a way that democracy may be guaranteed to the greatest possible extent.

2. In order to establish the appropriate articulation between the respective rights of such language communities and groups and the persons belonging to them, the quest for a satisfactory sociolinguistic balance must take into account various factors, in addition to their respective historical antecedents in the territory and their democratically expressed will. Among such factors, which may call for compensatory treatment aimed at restoring a balance, are the following: the coercive nature of the migrations which have led to the coexistence of the different communities and groups, and their degree of political, socioeconomic and cultural vulnerability.

Article 3
1. This Declaration considers the following to be inalienable personal rights which may be exercised in any situation:
the right to be recognized as a member of a language community;
the right to the use of one's own language both in private and in public;
the right to the use of one's own name;
the right to interrelate and associate with other members of one's language community of origin;
the right to maintain and develop one's own culture;
and all the other rights related to language which are recognized in the International Covenant on Civil and Political Rights of 16 December 1966 and the International Covenant on Economic, Social and Cultural Rights of the same date.

2. This Declaration considers that the collective rights of language groups, may include the following, in addition to the rights attributed to the members

of language groups in the foregoing paragraph, and in accordance with the conditions laid down in article 2.2:

the right for their own language and culture to be taught;

the right of access to cultural services;

the right to an equitable presence of their language and culture in the communications media;

the right to receive attention in their own language from government bodies and in socioeconomic relations.

3. The aforementioned rights of persons and language groups must in no way hinder the interrelation of such persons or groups with the host language community or their integration into that community. Nor must they restrict the rights of the host community or its members to the full public use of the community's own language throughout its territorial space.

Article 4

1. This Declaration considers that persons who move to and settle in the territory of another language community have the right and the duty to maintain an attitude of integration towards this community. This term is understood to mean an additional socialization of such persons in such a way that they may preserve their original cultural characteristics while sharing with the society in which they have settled sufficient references, values and forms of behaviour to enable them to function socially without greater difficulties than those experienced by members of the host community.

2. This Declaration considers, on the other hand, that assimilation, a term which is understood to mean acculturation in the host society, in such a way that the original cultural characteristics are replaced by the references, values and forms of behaviour of the host society, must on no account be forced or induced and can only be the result of an entirely free decision.

Article 5

This Declaration is based on the principle that the rights of all language communities are equal and independent of their legal status as official, regional or minority languages. Terms such as regional or minority languages are not used in this Declaration because, though in certain cases the recognition of regional or minority languages can facilitate the exercise of certain rights, these and other modifiers are frequently used to restrict the rights of language communities.

Article 6

This Declaration considers that a language cannot be considered specific to a territory merely on the grounds that it is the official language of the state or has been traditionally used within the territory for administrative purposes or for certain cultural activities.

TITLE ONE
General Principles

Article 7

1. All languages are the expression of a collective identity and of a distinct way of perceiving and describing reality and must therefore be able to enjoy the conditions required for their development in all functions.

2. All languages are collectively constituted and are made available within a community for individual use as tools of cohesion, identification, communication and creative expression.

Article 8

1. All language communities have the right to organize and manage their own resources so as to ensure the use of their language in all functions within

society.

2. All language communities are entitled to have at their disposal whatever means are necessary to ensure the transmission and continuity of their language.

Article 9

All language communities have the right to codify, standardize, preserve, develop and promote their linguistic system, without induced or forced interference.

Article 10

1. All language communities have equal rights.

2. This Declaration considers discrimination against language communities to be inadmissible, whether it be based on their degree of political sovereignty, their situation defined in social, economic or other terms, the extent to which their languages have been codified, updated or modernized, or on any other criterion.

3. All necessary steps must be taken in order to implement this principle of equality and to render it real and effective.

Article 11

All language communities are entitled to have at their disposal whatever means of translation into and from other languages are needed to guarantee the exercise of the rights contained in this Declaration.

Article 12

1. Everyone has the right to carry out all activities in the public sphere in

his/her language, provided it is the language specific to the territory where s/he resides.

2. Everyone has the right to use his/her language in the personal and family sphere.

Article 13
1. Everyone has the right to know the language specific to the territory in which s/he lives.

2. Everyone has the right to be polyglot and to know and use the language most conducive to his/her personal development or social mobility, without prejudice to the guarantees established in this Declaration for the public use of the language specific to the territory.

Article 14
The provisions of this Declaration cannot be interpreted or used to the detriment of any norm or practice deriving from the internal or international status of a language which is more favourable to its use within the territory to which it is specific.

SECOND TITLE
Overall linguistic régime

Section I
Public administration and official bodies

Article 15
1. All language communities are entitled to the official use of their language within their territory.

2. All language communities have the right for legal and administrative acts, public and private documents and records in public registers which are drawn up in the language of the territory to be valid and effective and no one can allege ignorance of this language.

Article 16
All language communities have the right to communicate in their own language with the central, territorial, local and supraterritorial services of the public authorities and of those administrative divisions which include the territory to which the language is specific.

Article 17
1. All language communities are entitled to have at their disposal and to obtain in their own language all official documents pertaining to relations which affect the territory to which the language is specific, whether such documents be in printed, machine-readable or any other form.

2. Forms and standard administrative documents, whether in printed, machine-readable or any other form, must be made available and placed at the disposal of the public in all territorial languages by the public authorities through the services which cover the territories to which each language is specific.

Article 18
1. All language communities have the right for laws and other legal provisions which concern them to be published in the language specific to the territory.

2. Public authorities who have more than one territorially historic language within their jurisdiction must publish all laws and other legal provisions of a general nature in each of these languages, whether or not their speakers

understand other languages.

Article 19
1. Representative Assemblies must have as their official language(s) the language(s) historically spoken in the territory they represent.

2. This right also applies to the languages of the communities established in geographically dispersed locations referred to in Article 1, Paragraph 4.

Article 20
1. Everyone has the right to use the language historically spoken in a territory, both orally and in writing, in the Courts of Justice located within that territory. The Courts of Justice must use the language specific to the territory in their internal actions and, if on account of the legal system in force within the state, the proceedings continue elsewhere, the use of the original language must be maintained.

2. Notwithstanding the above, everyone has the right to be tried in a language which s/he understands and can speak and to obtain the services of an interpreter free of charge.

Article 21
All language communities have the right for records in public registers to be drawn up in the language specific to the territory.

Article 22
All language communities have the right for documents authenticated by notaries public or certified by other authorized public servants to be drawn up in the language specific to the territory where the notary or other authorized public servant performs his/her functions.

Section II
Education

Article 23

1. Education must help to foster the capacity for linguistic and cultural self-expression of the language community of the territory where it is provided.

2. Education must help to maintain and develop the language spoken by the language community of the territory where it is provided.

3. Education must always be at the service of linguistic and cultural diversity and of harmonious relations between different language communities throughout the world.

4. Within the context of the foregoing principles, everyone has the right to learn any language.

Article 24

All language communities have the right to decide to what extent their language is to be present, as a vehicular language and as an object of study, at all levels of education within their territory: preschool, primary, secondary, technical and vocational, university, and adult education.

Article 25

All language communities are entitled to have at their disposal all the human and material resources necessary to ensure that their language is present to the extent they desire at all levels of education within their territory: properly trained teachers, appropriate teaching methods, text books, finance, buildings and equipment, traditional and innovative technology.

Article 26
All language communities are entitled to an education which will enable their members to acquire a full command of their own language, including the different abilities relating to all the usual spheres of use, as well as the most extensive possible command of any other language they may wish to know.

Article 27
All language communities are entitled to an education which will enable their members to acquire knowledge of any languages related to their own cultural tradition, such as literary or sacred languages which were formerly habitual languages of the community.

Article 28
All language communities are entitled to an education which will enable their members to acquire a thorough knowledge of their cultural heritage (history, geography, literature, and other manifestations of their own culture), as well as the most extensive possible knowledge of any other culture they may wish to know.

Article 29
1. Everyone is entitled to receive an education in the language specific to the territory where s/he resides.

2. This right does not exclude the right to acquire oral and written knowledge of any language which may be of use to him/her as an instrument of communication with other language communities.

Article 30
The language and culture of all language communities must be the subject of study and research at university level.

Section III
Proper names

Article 31

All language communities have the right to preserve and use their own system of proper names in all spheres and on all occasions.

Article 32

1. All language communities have the right to use place names in the language specific to the territory, both orally and in writing, in the private, public and official spheres.

2. All language communities have the right to establish, preserve and revise autochthonous place names. Such place names cannot be arbitrarily abolished, distorted or adapted, nor can they be replaced if changes in the political situation, or changes of any other type, occur.

Article 33

All language communities have the right to refer to themselves by the name used in their own language. Any translation into other languages must avoid ambiguous or pejorative denominations.

Article 34

Everyone has the right to the use of his/her own name in his/her own language in all spheres, as well as the right, only when necessary, to the most accurate possible phonetic transcription of his/her name in another writing system.

Section IV
Communications media and new technologies

Article 35
All language communities have the right to decide the extent to which their language is be present in all the communications media in their territory, whether local and traditional media, those with a wider scope, or those using more advanced technology, regardless of the method of dissemination or transmission employed.

Article 36
All language communities are entitled to have at their disposal all the human and material resources required in order to ensure the desired degree of presence of their language and the desired degree of cultural self-expression in the communications media in their territory: properly trained personnel, finance, buildings and equipment, traditional and innovative technology.

Article 37
All language communities have the right to receive, through the communications media, a thorough knowledge of their cultural heritage (history, geography, literature and other manifestations of their own culture), as well as the greatest possible amount of information about any other culture their members may wish to know.

Article 38
The languages and cultures of all language communities must receive equitable and non-discriminatory treatment in the communications media throughout the world.

Article 39
The communities described in Article 1, paragraphs 3 and 4, of this Declaration, and the groups mentioned in paragraph 5 of the same article, are entitled to an equitable representation of their language in the

communications media of the territory where they are established or where they migrate. This right is to be exercised in harmony with the rights of the other language groups or communities in the territory.

Article 40

In the field of information technology, all language communities are entitled to have at their disposal equipment adapted to their linguistic system and tools and products in their language, so as to derive full advantage from the potential offered by such technologies for publication, translation and information processing and for the dissemination of culture in general.

Section V
Culture

Article 41

1. All language communities have the right to use, maintain and foster their language in all forms of cultural expression.

2. All language communities must be able to exercise this right to the full without any community's space being subjected to hegemonic occupation by a foreign culture.

Article 42

All language communities have the right to full development within their own cultural sphere.

Article 43

All language communities are entitled to access to the works produced in their language.

Article 44
All language communities are entitled to access to intercultural programmes through the dissemination of adequate information, and to support for activities such as teaching the language to foreigners, translation, dubbing, post-synchronization and subtitling.

Article 45
All language communities have the right for the language specific to the territory to occupy a pre-eminent position in cultural events and services (libraries, videothèques, cinemas, theatres, museums, archives, folklore, cultural industries, and all other manifestations of cultural life).

Article 46
All language communities have the right to preserve their linguistic and cultural heritage, including its material manifestations, such as collections of documents, works of art and architecture, historic monuments and inscriptions in their own language.

Section VI
The socioeconomic sphere

Article 47
1. All language communities have the right to establish the use of their language in all socioeconomic activities within their territory.

2. All language communities are entitled to have at their disposal, in their own language, all the means necessary for the performance of their professional activities, such as documents and works of reference, instructions, forms and computer equipment, tools and products.

3. The use of other languages in this sphere can only be required in so far as it is justified by the nature of the professional activity involved. In no case can a more recently arrived language relegate or supersede the use of the language specific to the territory.

Article 48
1. All language communities have the right to use their language with full legal validity in economic transactions of all types, such as the sale and purchase of goods and services, banking, insurance, job contracts and others.

2. No clause in such private acts can exclude or restrict the use of a language in the territory to which it is specific.

3. All language communities are entitled to have the documents required for the performance of the above-mentioned operations at their disposal in their own language. Such documents include forms, cheques, contracts, invoices, receipts, delivery notes, order forms, and others.

Article 49
All language communities have the right to use their language in all types of socioeconomic organizations such as labour and union organizations, and employers', professional, trade and craft associations.

Article 50
1. All language communities have the right for their language to occupy a pre-eminent place in advertising, signs, external signposting, and all other elements that make up the image of the country.

2. All language communities have the right to receive full oral and written information in their own language on the products and services proposed by

commercial establishments in the territory, such as instructions for use, labels, lists of ingredients, advertising, guarantees and others.

3. All public signs and announcements affecting the safety of the public must be written at least in the language specific to the territory, in conditions which are not inferior to those of any other language.

Article 51
1. Everyone has the right to use the language specific to the territory in his/her relations with firms, commercial establishments and private bodies and to be served or receive a reply in the same language.

2. Everyone has the right, as a client, customer, consumer or user, to receive oral and written information in the language specific to the territory from establishments open to the public.

Article 52
Everyone has the right to carry out his/her professional activities in the language specific to the territory unless the functions inherent to the job require the use of other languages, as in the case of language teachers, translators or tourist guides.

ADDITIONAL DISPOSITIONS

First
The public authorities must take all appropriate steps to implement the rights proclaimed in this Declaration within their respective areas of jurisdiction. More specifically, international funds must be set up to foster the exercise of linguistic rights in communities which are demostrably lacking in resources. Thus the public authorities must provide the necessary support so that the

languages of the various communities may be codified, transcribed, taught, and used in the administration.

Second

The public authorities must ensure that the authorities, organizations and persons concerned are informed of the rights and correlative duties arising from this Declaration.

Third

The public authorities must establish, in the light of existing legislation, the sanctions arising from the violation of the linguistic rights laid down in this Declaration.

FINAL DISPOSITIONS

First

This Declaration proposes the creation of a Council of Languages within the United Nations Organization. The General Assembly of the United Nations Organization is to be responsible for setting up this Council, defining its functions and appointing its members, and for creating a body in international law to protect language communities in the exercise of the rights recognized in this Declaration.

Second

This Declaration recommends and promotes the creation of a World Commission on Linguistic Rights, a non-official, consultative body made up of representatives of non-governmental organizations and organizations working in the field of linguistic law.

Barcelona, June 1996

以上＜世界言語権宣言＞
(CIEMENホームページより：http:www.partal.com/ciemen)

● 英語を明らめよう

　「世界言語権宣言」の描写に垣間見られるこれまでの言語に関する人間の知見の集約をもとにして考えても、「total commitment」としての語学はいかに「あるがまま」に逆らおうとする行為なのかがよく観えてくると思います。
　ましてや「total commitment」としての語学を強制することなどは、まったくの狂気なのです。
　現在、日本では語学というと英語学習のことを思い浮かべる人が大多数のようです。幸か不幸かは別として、そのぐらい英語は日本人にとって身近な外（国）語です。そして、「英語をペラペラしゃべれるようになりたい」と思って英語学習に取り組んでいる人もかなり多いと思われます。
　それは当然です。誰だって労力や時間をかけて英語を学んでいる以上は「英語をペラペラしゃべれるようになりたい」と望むのが当然でしょう。
　しかし、もしもそのように望んでしまったら、ほとんどの人にとって語学は苦そのものになってしまいます。なぜならば、望みが叶わないものの一切は苦となるからです。
　適性と能力に恵まれたごく少数の人は、英語を学べば英語がペラペラにしゃべれるようになるかもしれません。しかしその望みが叶うまでに、英語をどのくらい学ばなければならないかを一言で表現すると「total commitment」なのですから、いかなる代償が必要なのかがもうお分かりかと思います。
　不可能ではありませんが、猛烈な苦を乗り越えなければならないのです。なんといっても、「あるがまま」に真っ向から逆らう行為なのですから仕方がありません。
　このような覚悟で英語を学んでいる人はそれでいいのです。でも、このような覚悟がいるということを知らずして、「英語をペラペラしゃべれるようになりたい」と望みつつ、英語を学んでいる人は不幸です。

そのような人は最初から
——英語を明らめませんか——
　本章の冒頭にも述べたように、「明らめ」は「諦め」ではありません。「あるがままをあるがままに受け入れる」ことが「明らめ」です。
　ですから、「英語を明らめよ」とは、
——あるがままの英語——
をよく見据えて下さい、と言っているのです。
　そうすると第1に明らかになることは、英語を相当に学んでも、英語がペラペラしゃべれるようにならないのは、あなたのせいではない、ということです。
　そのように明らめた上で、英語がペラペラしゃべれるようになりたい人は「total commitment」としての英語に相当の覚悟をもってのぞめばよいのです。
　そうでない人は、英語を学んで、英語が楽しめるようになればそれで充分ではありませんか。なんといってもあなたの母語は英語ではないのです。
——あるがままの自分を肯定する——
ことは、人間にとって非常に大切なことです。
　本来は（自然には）、英語学習は学習者が楽しむものであり、楽しくないような英語学習はやめればいいのです。
——英語は楽しむもの——
と明らめて、楽しむこと以外にこだわらないことをお勧めします。
　そして、くれぐれも、自らの主体性（自由）を奪われることなく、
——英語の奴隷状態から自らを解放する——
ことを心がけた上で、英語の学習を楽しまれることをお勧めします。
　著者は狂っているのかもしれません。とくに現代の全地球化（グローバル化）社会の規準、もしくは日本の政策が方向づけようとする規準や価値に照らせば、著者は完全に狂っています。
　現代日本社会の価値規準は、「経済効率」にあると言えるでしょう。すなわち、個人の幸福よりも企業や国家の利益が優先されている、ということです。
　企業戦士や国際人などという言葉に象徴される「世の中のために」働く「役に立つ」人材の育成を助長しているのです。「人としてあるがままの幸福」を追求する人は「役に立たない」として社会から抑圧されるのです。

「経済効率」や「能率至上主義」を「近代化」と称賛する日本人が多くいます。そのような人たちにとって「近代化」とは「国際化」でもあり、「国際化」の原動力は日本国民の英語力にある、ととらえている人が多いようです。ですから、英語ができる人は「役に立つ」という「世間の価値」が趨勢となるのです。

それだけならまだいいのですが、そのような「世間の価値」の奴隷となってしまった人が、もしも英語ができないと自分を「役立たず」と決めてしまうのです。完全な自己否定をしてしまうのです。

そもそも「世間の価値観」は時代の流れとともに変化します。つい50数年前までは「鬼畜米英」や「贅沢は敵・欲しがりません勝つまでは」や「英語＝敵性語」が常識とされ、その価値観への同化により国民と非国民を分別していた国家や社会が、今は「経済効率」や「内需拡大」や「国際化」や「英語コミュニケーション力」という価値によって「役に立つ」人と「役に立たない」人に分別しているのです。

そうすることが必要かどうかは、政治の判断です。善悪の問題を取り扱おうとしているのではありません。

ともあれ、「経済効率」や「能率」を優先する社会では、「競争」を育まなければなりません。「競争せよ」とは「他人を蹴落とせ」と言っていることにほかなりません。

ですから、現在の日本においては、他人を蹴落としてでも、企業や国家の経済利益のために、「total commitment」としての英語が重要視される風潮を生み出す社会になったのでしょう。

しかしながら、英語を外（国）語として「あるがまま」に受け入れるならば、このような風潮を生み出す日本社会こそ相当に狂っているのです。

著者が狂っているのか、日本社会が狂っているのかは読者諸賢のご判断に委ねます。

第2章　明らめの試み

● エル・ハジ・マリク・エル・シャバズ

So I say to you today, my friends, so even though we must face the difficulties of today and tomorrow, I still have a dream. It is a dream deeply rooted in the American dream that one day this nation will rise up and live out the true meaning of its creed — we hold these truths to be self-evident; that all men are created equal.

I have a dream that one day on the red hills of Georgia, sons of former slaves and sons of former slave-owners will be able to sit down together at the table of brotherhood.

I have a dream that one day, even the state of Mississippi, a state sweltering with the heat of injustice, sweltering with the heat of oppression, will be transformed into an oasis of freedom and justice.

I have a dream my four little children will one day live in a nation where they will not be judged by the color of their skin but by the content of their character. I have a dream today!

I have a dream that one day, down in Alabama, with its vicious racists, with its governor having his lips dripping with the words of interposition and nullification, that one day right here in Alabama, little black boys and black girls will be able to join hands with little white boys and white girls as sisters and brothers. I have a dream today!

I have a dream that one day every valley shall be exalted, every hill and mountain shall be made low, the rough places will be made plain, and crooked places will be made straight and the glory of the Lord shall be revealed and all flesh shall see it together.

(Washington 1992: 104-5)

「米国における公民権運動の代表的人物は？」と聞かれて、キング牧師 (Martin Luther King, Jr.) の名前を挙げない人はほとんどいないでしょう。公民権運動のことをまったく知らなくても、キング牧師という名前ぐらいは聞いたことがあるという人も多いかもしれません。上の引用は、キング牧師の演説の中でも最も有名なものの1つ「I Have a Dream」演説の一部です。この演説では、その名のとおり「私には夢がある」ということばが何度も繰り返されます。米国で黒人が白人と同等の自由と権利を獲得し、お互いがお互いを尊重しながら共に生きられる、そんな日が来ることを彼は夢見ていたのです。今から30数年前のことです。

　ちょうど同じ時期、キング牧師（西暦1928年、ジョージア州、アトランタ生まれ）の「夢」に対し、「私には悪夢が見える」と叫んだアフリカ系米国人がいました。それがエル・ハジ・マリク・エル・シャバズ（El-Hajj Malik El-Shabazz）、別名マルコムX（西暦1925年、ネブラスカ州、オマハ生まれ）です。

Well, I am one who doesn't believe in deluding myself. I'm not going to sit at your table and watch you eat, with nothing on my plate, and call myself a diner. Sitting at the table doesn't make you a diner, unless you eat some of what's on that plate. Being here in America doesn't make you an American. Being born here in America doesn't make you an American. Why, if birth made you American, you wouldn't need any legislation, you wouldn't need any amendments to the Constitution, you wouldn't be faced with civil-rights filibustering in Washington, D.C., right now. They don't have to pass civil-rights legislation to make a Polack an American.

No, I'm not an American. I'm one of the 22 million black people who are the victims of Americanism. One of the 22 million black people who are the victims of democracy, nothing but disguised hypocrisy. So, I'm not standing here speaking to you as an American, or a patriot, or a flag-saluter, or a flag-waver ― no, not I. I'm speaking as a victim of this American system. And I see America through the eyes of the victim. I don't see any American dream; I see an American nightmare.

(Breitman 1990: 26)

　スパイク・リー監督の映画『マルコムX』(1992) をきっかけに、西暦1990年代になって米国では再びマルコムXが脚光を浴びているそうです。1960年代に活躍したマルコムXが90年代になぜ再び「ヒーロー」とみなされるのでしょうか。なぜキング牧師ではないのでしょうか。それは、90年代に至ってもXが注目される背景が米国に存在することを意味します。

　米国は、西暦1776年の独立宣言で、平等、人権、民主主義思想を高らかに謳いながら成立したにもかかわらず、その後約1世紀にわたって奴隷制を維持し、奴隷解放後も人種による差別政策を根強く残していました。その状況下1950年代から60年代にかけてキング牧師らを中心とする公民権運動が盛り上がりを見せ、1964年に制定された公民権法、翌年成立した投票権法、そして90年代に至るまでの積極的差別是正措置などにより、アフリカ系米国人をはじめとするいわゆる少数派の地位は格段に改善されたとも言われています。それにもかかわらず、たとえば1992年にはロサンゼルス市南部の黒人居住地区、サウスセントラルで暴動が起こり、死者58人、負傷者2,380人、損壊家屋約2,000軒という惨事になっています。この暴動はさらにラスベガス、サンフランシスコ、シアトル、アトランタにまで飛び火しました。

　もっともこの一連の暴動は、四半世紀前に見られた「白人対黒人」という単純な図式ではなく、特にロサンゼルス暴動においては、ヒスパニック系、韓国系の少数民族なども複雑に絡んだものとなっていたようです。いずれにせよ、このような大規模暴動が起こる土壌がいまだに米国には存在していることは確かです。公民権運動の後、政治をはじめとする多くの分野で活躍するアフリカ系米国人が増えたことは事実ですが、その一方で貧しい人もむしろ増えているという指摘もあります。次の引用は、米国史研究者、猿谷要氏の『歴史物語アフリカ系アメリカ人』からです。

・・・ブラック・アンダークラスとよばれる黒人の貧困層は少しも減らないばかりか、80年代のレーガン政権以来、むしろ増加していることも事実である。豊かな階層はますます富み、貧しい階層はますます貧困になって、貧富の差が拡大したことは、多くの人々によって指摘されている通りである。

その原因は1世帯当たり中間収入（1993年）の比較が示している通り、人種による差別ばかりでなく、むしろこの国の本源的な社会構造によると言うべきだろう。

白人	31,241ドル
黒人	19,533ドル
ヒスパニック	22,886ドル
アジア・太平洋	38,347ドル

世界一豊かなはずのアメリカには、貧困どころか飢餓が存在している。資源が乏しく、大戦後灰の中から立ち上がった日本のような国でも解決している飢餓の問題が、アメリカではまだ解決されず、黒人や先住アメリカ人（インディアン）などが、そのなかに大勢含まれているのだ。(2000: 352-53)

米国でマルコムXが多くの人に再び注目されるようになった背景にはこのような状況が存在し、彼を支持する人の多くは、貧困の「悪循環」から逃れられない黒人大衆層であることが想像されます。

日本においても、スパイク・リー監督の映画でその名が知られるようになりましたが、映画を見て内容に興味を持たれた方はともかく、「パブリック・エネミー」などのラップ音楽人気と絡んで、「X」の文字入り帽子、Tシャツといったファッションとしてのみ受け入れた人も多かったように思われます。欧米の「流行」に日本の若者が飛びつく（飛びつかされる）ことはしばしば見られることで、それ自体を批判したところであまり意味はありません。若い世代に限らず多くの日本人が、欧米特に米国に対しては、政治、経済、科学技術、文化（行動様式・価値観）の様々な分野で先進、自由、高度、洗練などの「良い」印象を持っているようですから、若者が米国の流行を追うことも日本人一般の持つ意識の現れの一例にすぎません。

しかし、せっかく知られるようになったマルコムXの名前をファッションだ

けに終わらせるのは非常に残念な気がします。時間を超えて注目される彼のことばの中には、我々が米国を、そして場合によっては我々自身の国や世界を見る別の視点を与えてくれる何かがあると著者は考えるからです。

さらに言うと、前章で述べた「明らめ」の一体現者、一実践者の姿が彼の中に見いだせるのです。言語や文化そして英語の話からいきなりマルコムXの話に移り、唐突に思われたかもしれませんが、この章では、自分自身を「明らめ」、他者に対しても「明らめ」をすすめようと試みたマルコムXの視点を、彼の演説や自伝を通して、適宜キング牧師らの視点と比較しながら検証してみたいと思います。

さて、まず先の引用から見てみましょう。マルコムXは、そもそも米国の「民主主義」などのイデオロギー（「自由」や「平等」も含めて）は「偽善」であると考えます。「黒人」は米国で生まれたとしても「米国人」にはなれない、本当に「米国人」というなら公民権法案も憲法修正条項も必要ではないはずなのだと。

確かに米国は建国当初から「すべての人間の平等」を唱えている国です。次の引用は、キング牧師も「I Have a Dream」演説で引用していた『アメリカ合衆国独立宣言』（西暦1776年7月4日）の一節です。

> We hold these truths to be self-evident, that all men are created equal, that they are endowed by their Creator with certain unalienable Rights, that among these are Life, Liberty, and the pursuit of Happiness.

しかし現実には、平等なのは「all men」ではなく、「all white men」であり、アフリカ系米国人（黒人）や米国先住民（アメリカ・インディアン）には適用されなかったと言って差し支えないでしょう。奴隷貿易は禁止になったとはいえ奴隷制は19世紀後半まで続き、奴隷解放後も人種隔離、政治的権利剥奪、経済的搾取は相変わらず行われましたし、米国先住民の迫害は「西部開拓」の歴史と共にありました。

自由、平等そして民主主義を標榜しながら、黒人の現実はまったく異なる米国という国、さらに言えば白人の権力構造そのものを、マルコムXは糾弾した

のです。キング牧師も米国建国の理想が実現されていないことは常に指摘していましたから、この点ではマルコムXもマーチン・キングも同じでした。基本的に異なるのは、キングが米国白人の価値観（意識）を変えられるという「希望（夢）」を持っていたのに対し、Xは変えられないという「明らめ（悪夢）」が強かった点だと思われます。その結果、キングが「統合主義（integrationism）」を採ったのに対し、Xは「黒人民族主義（black nationalism、特に活動初期には具体的な「分離主義」）」を主張したのです。そして運動の方針として、キングの「非暴力（nonviolence）」に対し、Xは「自衛（self-defense）」を強調します。

　これらの違いには、キングが「キリスト教徒」、Xが「イスラム教徒」であったこと、さらにはキングが比較的恵まれた家庭環境で育ったのに対し、Xが家庭崩壊そして多くの犯罪行為を経験していることなども反映されているようです。以下、常に彼の思想の中心概念となっていた「黒人民族主義」、闘争手段の基本方針である「自衛」、黒人闘争の解決策として最終的に到達した概念である「人権」の順に、その意味の解説、あるいはその意義の考察（明らめ）を試みたいと思います。

● 黒人民族主義（black nationalism）

　当時、アフリカ系米国人の間に、米国にいる黒人は究極的には故郷アフリカに帰還するか、あるいは米国でアフリカ系米国人の人口比に応じた土地を勝ち取り独立するべきであるという目標を共有する宗教団体が存在しました（現在も存在します）。「イスラムの民（Nation of Islam）」と呼ばれるアフリカ系米国人のみで構成されるイスラム教団体がそれです。マルコムXの名が世間に知られるようになったのは、この「イスラムの民」の筆頭幹部、ないしは教団の代表者イライジャ・ムハマドの代弁者としてでした。アフリカ帰還、北米大陸内での黒人国家または黒人州の独立という教団の目標の前提として、彼らは「自民族に対する誇り」を何よりも重要なものと位置づけました。マルコムXは晩年この教団を脱退することになるのですが、教団員であったころはもちろん脱

退後もこの「自民族に対する誇り」を常に強調し続けました。
　彼が「イスラムの民」の教えに出合ったのは刑務所の中でした。それまでの彼の経歴は、幼い頃父を殺され（事故死という説もある）一家離散、その後施設を転々とし、学校は8学年で中退、ボストン、続いてニューヨークのハーレムに移り、ハスラー（酒の密売、麻薬売買、ポン引き、博打、窃盗などで生計を立てるやくざ者）へと成長、宝石店に盗みに入ったところを逮捕、投獄というものでした。白人のために悲惨な目に遭わされた子供時代を過ごしたにもかかわらず、ハスラー時代の彼は白人とうまくつきあい、コンク・ヘア（巻き毛を薬で直毛にするヘア・スタイル）にするなど、無意識的に白人に近づき同化しようとしていたのです。そんな彼にとり、刑務所で知った「イスラムの民」の教えは衝撃的でした。

　'The true knowledge', reconstructed much more briefly than I received it, was that history had been 'whitened' in the white man's history books, and that the black man had been 'brainwashed for hundreds of years'. Original Man was black, in the continent called Africa where the human race had emerged on the planet Earth.
　The black man, original man, built great empires and civilizations and cultures while the white man was still living on all fours in caves. 'The devil white man', down through history, out of his devilish nature, had pillaged, murdered, raped, and exploited every race of man not white.
　Human history's greatest crime was the traffic in black flesh when the devil white man went into Africa and murdered and kidnapped to bring to the West in chains, in slave ships, millions of black men, women and children, who were worked and beaten and tortured as slaves.
　The devil white man cut these black people off from all knowledge of their own language, religion, and past culture, until the black man in America was the earth's only race of people who had absolutely no knowledge of his true identity.
　In one generation, the black slave women in America had been raped by

the slavemaster white man until there had begun to emerge a homemade, handmade, brainwashed race that was no longer even of its true color, that no longer even knew its true family names. The slavemaster forced his family name upon this rape-mixed race, which the slavemaster began to call 'the Negro'.

This 'Negro' was taught of his native Africa that it was peopled by heathen, black savages, swinging like monkeys from trees. This 'Negro' accepted this along with every other teaching of the slavemaster that was designed to make him accept and obey and worship the white man.

And where the religion of every other people on earth taught its believers of a God with whom they could identify, a God who at least looked like one of their own kind, the slavemaster injected his Christian religion into this 'Negro'. This 'Negro' was taught to worship an alien God having the same blond hair, pale skin and blue eyes as the slavemaster.

This religion taught the 'Negro' that black was a curse. It taught him to hate everything black, including himself. It taught him that everything white was good, to be admired, respected and loved. It brainwashed this 'Negro' to think he was superior if his complexion showed more of the white pollution of the slavemaster. This white man's Christian religion further deceived and brainwashed this 'Negro' to always turn the other cheek, and grin, and scrape, and bow, and be humble, and to sing, and to pray and to take whatever was dished out by the devilish white man; and to look for his pie in the sky, and for his heaven in the hereafter, while right here on earth the slavemaster white man enjoyed *his* heaven.

(Haley & X 1965: 256-7)

「イスラムの民」は、米国の神学者、ジェイムズ・H．コーン氏によると、1930年にデトロイトの黒人共同体においてウォーレス・D・ファードによって設立された国内産の「黒人宗教」であり、世界大のイスラム共同体との直接的歴史的関係はほとんど存在しないようです。

... The doctrines and practices of traditional Islam were secondary to the main themes of Elijah Muhammad's Nation: the rejection of Christianity as the white man's religion, and the affirmation of Elijah Muhammad's interpretation of Islam as the "natural religion of the black man," this interpretation having been given to Muhammad by Allah ("in the person of Wallace D. Fard") for the purpose of restoring the self-esteem and self-confidence of the "Lost-Found Nation of so-called Negroes in the West."

(Cone 1991: 161)

　東方のイスラムとの関係はともかく、マルコムXにとっては、「イスラムの民」の当時の指導者、イライジャ・ムハマドの教えが「真実」だと実感できたことは間違いありません。服役中、教えに出合って間もなくマルコムXはその組織に入会し、刑務所の中で本という本を読み漁ります。また辞書を丸ごと手書きでノートに写し取ることなどを通して語彙と知識の蓄積を図り、刑務所内での討論会などにも積極的に参加しました。その過程で彼は「自民族への誇り」に目覚め、悟ったのです。黒人は輝かしい歴史、文明を持つ民族であること、アフリカ系米国人は白人によって米国へ家畜のように運び込まれ、名前、言語、歴史、文化、宗教すべてを奪われたこと、さらに自分たちは、白人の名前、言語、歴史、文化、宗教を押し付けられ、白人のすべてが優れ、黒人のすべてが劣ったものであると洗脳されてしまったということを。そしてそのようなことが平気でできる白人はすべて「悪魔」であることを。

　スパイク・リー監督の『マルコムX』を見られた方はご記憶にあるかもしれませんが、映画の中に、「黒」と「白」の色に関係する、刑務所内でのエピソードがありました。2つご紹介しましょう。

　1つは、英語という言語における「white」と「black」の定義に関するものです。マルコムは服役中、同じ刑務所にいた「イスラムの民」の団員に勧められ、辞書の「white」と「black」の項を読みます。「white」の語義の多くが肯定的な意味合いを持ち、「black」はその逆に否定的なものがほとんどであることを彼はそこで見つけ愕然としてしまうのです。当時の辞書とは多少語義が変わっているかもしれませんが、現在の辞書を試しに見てみましょう。

white (*adjective*)

    1 a : free from color **b** : of the color of new snow or milk; *specifically* : of the color white **c** : light or pallid in color <*white* hair> <lips *white* with fear> **d** : lustrous pale gray : **SILVERY**; *also* : made of silver

    2 a : being a member of a group or race characterized by reduced pigmentation and usually specifically distinguished from persons belonging to groups marked by black, brown, yellow, or red skin coloration **b** : of, relating to, characteristic of, or consisting of white people **c** : marked by upright fairness

    3 : free from spot or blemish: as **a** (1) : free from moral impurity : **INNOCENT** (2) : marked by the wearing of white by the woman as a symbol of purity <a *white* wedding> **b** : unmarked by writing or printing **c** : not intended to cause harm <a *white* lie> <*white* magic> **d** : **FAVORABLE**, **FORTUNATE** <one of the *white* days of his life — Sir Walter Scott>

    4 a : wearing or habited in white **b** : marked by the presence of snow : **SNOWY** <a *white* Christmas>

    5 a : heated to the point of whiteness **b** : notably ardent : **PASSIONATE** <*white* fury>

    6 a : conservative or reactionary in political outlook and action **b** : instigated or carried out by reactionary forces as a counterrevolutionary measure <a *white* terror>

    7 : of, relating to, or constituting a musical tone quality characterized by a controlled pure sound, a lack of warmth and color, and a lack of resonance

    8 : consisting of a wide range of frequencies — used of light, sound, and electromagnetic radiation

black (*adjective*)

    1 a : of the color black **b** (1) : very dark in color <his face was *black* with rage> (2) : having a very deep or low register <a bass with a *black* voice> (3) : **HEAVY**, **SERIOUS** <the play was a *black* intrigue>

    2 a : having dark skin, hair, and eyes : **SWARTHY** <the *black* Irish> **b** (1) *often capitalized* : of or relating to any of various population groups having dark pigmentation of the skin <*black* Americans> (2) : of or relating to the Afro-American people or their culture <*black* literature> <a *black* college> <*black* pride> <*black* studies> (3) : typical or representative of the most readily attended parts of black culture <tried to play *blacker* jazz>

3 : dressed in black

4 : DIRTY, SOILED <hands *black* with grime>

5 a : characterized by the absence of light <a *black* night> **b** : reflecting or transmitting little or no light <*black* water> **c** : served without milk or cream <*black* coffee>

6 a : thoroughly sinister or evil : **WICKED** <a *black* deed> **b** : indicative of condemnation or discredit <got a *black* mark for being late>

7 : connected with or invoking the supernatural and especially the devil <*black* magic>

8 a : very sad, gloomy, or calamitous <*black* despair> **b** : marked by the occurrence of disaster <*black* Friday>

9 : characterized by hostility or angry discontent : **SULLEN** <*black* resentment filled his heart>

10 *chiefly British* : subject to boycott by trade-union members as employing or favoring nonunion workers or as operating under conditions considered unfair by the trade union

11 a *of propaganda* : conducted so as to appear to originate within an enemy country and designed to weaken enemy morale **b** : characterized by or connected with the use of black propaganda <*black* radio>

12 : characterized by grim, distorted, or grotesque satire <*black* humor>

13 : of or relating to covert intelligence operations <*black* government programs>

(*Merriam-Webster's Collegiate Dictionary* (2000) Merriam-Webster On-line http://www.m-w.com/home.htm)

こうして見ると、今でも英語の「white」は肯定的な語義を、「black」は否定的な語義を多く持っていることがよく分かります。ついでながら、日本語の「白い」と「黒い」ではどうでしょうか。『広辞苑』（第5版）で見てみましょう。

「白い」
①白色である。白である。雪のような色をしている。
②どの色にも染めてない。また、何も書いてない。
③明るい。輝いている。
④経験にとぼしい。野暮である。
⑤潔白である。正しい。

「黒い」
①墨のような色である。
②濃紫・褐色・にび色などの、黒っぽい色にいう。
③日に焼けている。
④よごれている。きたない。
⑤悪い。不正である。公明でなく悪心がある。

　日本語でも白に肯定的、黒に否定的意味合いがありますが、英語に比べるとそのイメージの差は遙かに小さいようです。たとえば日本語の「白い」には「野暮である」という意味も含まれています。他にもいくつか白や黒が含まれた語句を挙げてみましょう。同じく『広辞苑』です。

「黒帯」①黒色の帯。②柔道・空手で、有段者が用いる黒色の帯。
「黒面」①黒い顔。黒色の顔。②実直。誠実。
「黒白衣」墨染の衣ころもと平常の衣服。僧侶と俗人。
「黒表」（blacklistの訳語）要注意人物の一覧表。ブラック‐リスト。
「黒っぽい」①黒みをおびている。②玄人くろうとらしい。
「白帯」①白色の帯。②柔道などで、段位のない者が締める白色の帯。

「白ける」①白くなる。②負色(まけいろ)になる。ぐあいが悪くなる。間が悪くなる。③興がさめる。気まずくなる。

「白白しい」①いかにも白く見える。白い。②興ざめである。あじきない。③しらばくれている。

「白痴」知能がいちじるしく劣っていること。また、医学で精神薄弱の程度が最も甚だしい状態をいった語。

「白鬼」①しろおに。②売春婦の異称。

　日本語における黒は必ずしも「悪い」、「不正な」意味合いだけでなく、むしろ肯定的な意味で使われる例も比較的多いように思われます。逆に「白」は武道などの「白帯」などにも見られるように、「劣った」意味をも持っていると言えます。

　言語が「分別」の道具としての機能を持つことは前章まででお分かりだと思いますが、元々アングロサクソン民族の言語である「英語」が、マルコムＸの気づいたように、その民族（白人）にとって都合の良い「分別の装置」を内在していることは充分考えられることです。もちろんこのような現象は、言語と文化のかかわりから考えるとどの自然言語においても不可避なことではあります。

　もう1つのエピソードは、「白人のキリスト教」にかかわるものです。刑務所で『聖書』の講義を担当していたキリスト教白人牧師に対して、マルコムＸは問いかけます。「使徒たちの肌の色は？」、「彼らはヘブライ人、イエスもヘブライ人、歴史的に見て当時のヘブライ人は肌の色が白ではないはずだ」と。牧師は部屋にあるイエスの肖像を指さし、「神（イエス）は白人だ」と反論します。それに対しマルコムＸは、描かれた神（イエス）は白人が作り上げたイメージに過ぎないこと、その証拠として『黙示録』には「イエスの髪は羊毛状で足の色は真鍮色」と書いてあることを指摘します。その時彼が引用したのは次の部分です。（いずれも *The BibleGateway* のホームページより引用。http://bible.gospelcom. net/bible?language= english）

Revelation 1:14-15 :: *King James Version (KJV)*
14 His head and his hairs were white like wool, as white as snow; and his eyes were as a flame of fire;
15 And his feet like unto fine brass, as if they burned in a furnace; and his voice as the sound of many waters.

神（イエス）の足が「炉で精錬されて輝く真鍮のようだ」と確かに書かれています。ただ髪の毛に関しては、「羊毛状」、即ち「巻き毛状」というより「羊毛や雪のように白い」という描き方です。しかも白いのは、「頭と髪」となっています。英語の「head」が首から上全体を指すとすれば顔も含まれることになりますが、英語訳された聖書の他の版では次のようなものもあります。

Revelation 1:14-15 :: *Worldwide English Version*
14 The hair on his head was white like sheep's hair, white as snow. His eyes shone like a flame of fire.
15 His feet shone like fine brass that has been made pure by fire. His voice was like the sound of much water flowing.

この版によると、羊毛のように白いのは「頭髪」に限定され顔は含まれません。そうすると足の色の類推から肌の色全体が真鍮色と考えて不自然ではないといえます。ちなみに（キリスト教で言う）『旧約聖書、ダニエル書』(10:6)では、主（神）の「腕と足」が「みがきあげた青銅のようだ」とも書いてあります。実際にイエスや使徒たちの肌の色はどうであったかという問題が、神学、歴史学等の研究において確定されない以上、聖書のこれらの記述は、少なくともイエス（神）も使徒たちも「白い肌」であるとは言えないことの根拠となり得ます。マルコムXにそれを指摘され、白人牧師は何も言えなくなってしまいます。

映画のこれら2つのエピソードは当然ながら脚色があります。たとえば2つ目のエピソードに登場するキリスト教牧師は自伝によるとハーバード神学校の学生ですが、彼との対話に聖書の引用は出てきません。「最初のヘブライ人が黒人だった」と言うだけで、学生は認めざるを得なかったようです。

こうしたエピソードにも見られるように、白人に彼らの言語や宗教を通して洗脳されてきた自分の価値観をまさしく180度転換させたマルコムXは、出所後「イスラムの民」の意見、所信などの公表を担当する代表的人物へと成長していきます。その過程において、彼はアフリカ系米国人、特に経済的・社会的下層階級にある黒人聴衆の意識の転換を図ります。奴隷制時代から長い間強化されてきた白人中心の価値観の中で、決してアフリカ系米国人が口にできなかったであろうことをまったく躊躇なく彼は叫んだのです。白人のことを「悪魔(devil)、生まれながら邪悪な存在(evil by nature)、狼、狐、犬、蛇」などと呼び、「美しい」と黒人が思い込まされてきた白人の白い肌を「pale（血の気がない、血色が悪い、青白い） skin」、白人の細長い鼻を「dog-like（犬のような） nose」、他にも「bad-smelling（臭い）」、「sickly-looking（青ざめて病的に見える）」などと形容しました。言語の持つ「分別の機能」を逆に利用したわけです。これほどまでに白人を見下す表現は、キリスト教白人が今まで歴史上行ってきた「悪行」を示すことによって説得力を持ってきます。たとえば奴隷制、奴隷貿易です。

...'I know you don't realize the enormity, the horrors, of the so-called *Christian* white man's crime....

'Not even in the *Bible* is there such a crime! God in His wrath struck down with *fire* the perpetrators of *lesser* crimes! *One hundred million* of us black people! Your grandparents! Mine! *Murdered* by this white man. To get fifteen million of us here to make us his slaves, on the way he murdered one hundred million! I wish it was possible for me to show you the sea bottom in those days — the black bodies, the blood, the bones broken by boots and clubs! The pregnant black women who were thrown overboard if they got too sick! Thrown overboard to the sharks that had learned that following these slave ships was the way to grow fat!

'Why, the white man's raping of the black race's woman began right on those slave ships! The blue-eyed devil could not even wait until he got them here! Why, brothers and sisters, civilized mankind has never know such an orgy of greed and lust and murder ...'

(Haley & X 1965: 311-2)

　主に16世紀から19世紀にかけて行われた奴隷貿易で、実際どれくらいの数の黒人がアフリカ大陸からアメリカ大陸へ運ばれたか正確には分かりません。たとえば本田創造氏は、エドワード・E・ダンバーの推定（総計1,400万人近く）とW・E・B・デュボイスの言葉（「1人の黒人を新大陸にもたらすまでには5人の黒人が途中で死んだ」）を基準に、「総計7,000万人のアフリカ黒人が無惨にも母国から奪い去られたことになる（1991: 28）」としていますから、マルコムXの「1億人」というのは多く見積もりすぎで事実とは異なると言えるのかもしれません。しかし、実際の数字が仮に10分の1であったとしても1,000万ですから「厖大な数字」であることに変わりはないですし、20世紀半ばのアフリカ系米国人のほとんどがアフリカから連れ去られた「奴隷」の子孫であり、奴隷制が廃止された後も人種隔離、経済的搾取等の対象であり続けたことは「事実」です。

　彼の語る「白人悪魔説」は、奴隷制だけでは終わりません。奴隷制が終わってからも「悪魔」がいかにしてアフリカ系米国人を2級市民（second class citizen）の地位に押し込めてきたか、すなわち米国内における黒人に対する白人の権力構造を告発します。

What makes the so-called Negro unable to stand on his own two feet? He has no self-confidence. He has no self-confidence in his own race, because the white man destroyed your and my past. Destroyed our knowledge of our culture. And by having destroyed it, now we don't know we have any achievements, any accomplishments, and as long as you can be convinced that you never did anything, you can never do anything

　...

　This is why the white man, he tells his little children about George Washington, Abraham Lincoln. All of these are white heroes, but we are never taught about any black heroes. Only someone we're shown in history

is my grandfather who was picking cotton.
   ...

   Cotton picking don't move me, no. But when it comes to teaching the black people something about the great black men who stood their ground, who were scientists, who were civilizers, who were fathers of culture and civilization, the white man has shrewdly written that role out of the textbook. And today, the affect it has on you and me, we don't think we can stand on our own two feet.
   (*Music and Dialogue from the Original Soundtrack of the Motion Picture : Malcolm X* 1972)

彼がここで指摘しているのは、宗教も含む教育の問題です。世界および米国の歴史上（白人社会の価値観においても）「偉大」とみなされる功績を残した多くの黒人が存在するにもかかわらず、その名は抜け目なく教科書から排除されているというのです。そのためアフリカ系米国人は、自分の親が、自分の祖父母が、自分の祖先が、誇るべきことを何一つ成し遂げていないのだと信じ込まされ、自分自身も自分の足で立ち上がる気など持てなくなるのだと。

米国白人の悪業、権力構造を暴露することにより、マルコムXは特に白人の間で「憎悪の教師」としてその名が知られるようになっていきますが、彼自身は自分が「憎しみ」を説いているとはまったく考えてなかったのです。彼に言わせれば、「黒人に白人を憎むな」と説くことは、「自分の親を殺した人間を憎むな」、「自分をレイプした人間を憎むな」と説くことと同じことになります。多少劇的効果を加えたとしても、彼が黒人聴衆に伝えたことは、アフリカ系米国人にほとんど知らせられることのない米国白人の「あるがままの姿」であり、そしてその白人に洗脳されている米国黒人の「あるがままの姿」だったのです。彼は、黒人大衆に対して「白人を憎め」とは言いません。「あるがままの姿を見ろ」と言います。さらに黒人の自助努力、自己改善を訴えます。

   We wake up, we clean up and we stand up. And once we can stand up like a man on our own feet, we stop begging the white man and we stop apologizing to the white man. We stop compromising with the white man. Then the world will look at us with recognition and respect. But as long as you run around here wearing the white man's name, bragging that you one of the Jones, or one of the Browns, or one of the Smiths. As long as you're running around bragging about your part in this so-called American democracy, then you'll always be looked down upon as a chump by the white man. You never will be given recognition nor respect. Your problem will continue to go unsolved and we'll still be in the same rut, or ditch, a thousand years from now that we're in right now.

(同上から引用)

　この内容は彼の名前「X」とも関係してきます。彼の本名（米国の出生証明にある姓名）は「Malcolm Little」、つまり姓は「Little」です。「X」を名乗るようになったのは、「イスラムの民」に入会してからです。アフリカから奴隷として米国に運び込まれた黒人の名前は、奴隷所有者である白人に与えられたものです。その子供や孫たちは、名は親から与えられますが、姓の方は奴隷主がつけたものをそのまま引き継いできたわけです。「イスラムの民」は、アフリカ系米国人の根源をアフリカに求めますから、奴隷主につけられた姓は否定するのです。そして永久に分からない自分のアフリカの家族の姓を象徴するものとして「X」を名乗り、神自身が聖なる名前を与えてくれるまでそれを使っていくというのが彼らの方針でした。

　余談になりますが、彼は晩年メッカ巡礼を行ったころから「マリク・エル・シャバズ」という名もしばしば使うようになります。これは正統派イスラム教徒としての名であり、彼の墓碑銘にはこの名に「エル・ハジ（正式の巡礼の時期にメッカ巡礼を遂げたイスラム教徒に与えられる称号）」を冠して「エル・ハジ・マリク・エル・シャバズ」と記されているようです。マルコムXの死後その家族は、彼の「主観的自己認識（アイデンティティ）」がこの名前にあると解釈したのでしょう。「マルコム・リトル」でも「マルコムX」でもなく「エル・ハジ・マリク・エル・シャバズ」こそが彼自身であったと考えることは、彼の言動から見ても妥当であると言えます。彼の妻や子供たちも「シャバズ」をそ

の後名乗っていますが、彼らもやはりその名前に自らの主観的自己認識を込めているに違いありません。

　主観的自己認識の基礎となる本来の名前、言語、宗教、歴史、文化をすべて自分たちから奪い取った白人に媚び、請い、謝り、同化することをやめ、アフリカ系米国人としてでなくアフリカ黒人としての誇りと自信を取り戻す。理想的には祖国アフリカへの帰還あるいは米国の土地内での黒人共同体として独立（州または国家として白人からの「分離（separation）」）を考えるが、当面米国内で生きなければならない以上、白人に助けを求めず自分たちで精神的にも経済的にも独立して生活する。これが、黒人大衆に向かってマルコムXが訴え続けた「黒人民族主義」であったようです。

　もちろん彼は「イスラムの民」を代表して、すなわちイライジャ・ムハマドの代弁者として語っていたわけですから、解釈やことば自体は彼のものとはいえ、思想そのものは彼独自のものではなくイライジャ・ムハマドの教えの範囲を出ることはありませんでした。晩年、彼は「イスラムの民」から離れ、思想的にも多少変化がありました。特にメッカ巡礼、アフリカ諸国訪問を終え、世界大のスンニ派イスラムの視点を持つようになってからは、「白人悪魔説」を撤回します。しかし、基本的にこの「黒人民族主義」、特に「自民族に対する誇り」が彼の活動の中心的主題であることに変わりはありませんでした。

● 自衛（self-defense）

　米国南部、アラバマ州モントゴメリーにおけるバスボイコット運動に始まる公民権闘争は、黒人キリスト教団体を中心に進められました。その代表的指導者であるキング牧師は、運動の方針として「非暴力直接行動（non-violent direct action）」を繰り返し主張しました。デモ行進や座り込み（sit-in）などの抗議行動をする場合はもちろん、KKKなどの白人民族主義過激派に見せしめのため同胞を殺されたり、教会を爆破されたとき、あるいは自分自身が刺されたり、自宅を爆破されたときでさえ、彼がこの「非暴力（non-violence）」の態度を変えることはなく、多くの公民権運動家たちも彼に従いました。

「非暴力」の理念は、「非暴力、不服従」を標語に掲げ大英帝国からインドを解放したマハトマ・ガンジーの思想に影響を受けたものですが、キリスト教の聖書にもその根拠を求めることができます。『マタイの福音書』第5章39節の中に「悪い者に手向かってはいけません。あなたの右の頬を打つような者には、左の頬も向けなさい」とあります。これはキリスト教でいう『旧約聖書』で認められていた「同害報復」の教えを否定する文脈で出てきます。見比べてみましょう。

Leviticus 24:19-21 :: *King James Version (KJV)*　(『旧約聖書、レビ記』)
　19 And if a man cause a blemish in his neighbour; as he hath done, so shall it be done to him;
　20 Breach for breach, eye for eye, tooth for tooth: as he hath caused a blemish in a man, so shall it be done to him again.
　21 And he that killeth a beast, he shall restore it: and he that killeth a man, he shall be put to death.

Matthew 5:38-40 :: *King James Version (KJV)*　(『新約聖書、マタイの福音書』)
　38 Ye have heard that it hath been said, An eye for an eye, and a tooth for a tooth:
　39 But I say unto you, That ye resist not evil: but whosoever shall smite thee on thy right cheek, turn to him the other also.
　40 And if any man will sue thee at the law, and take away thy coat, let him have thy cloak also.

　『旧約』では「骨折には骨折、目には目、歯には歯」というように相手にされたことと同じだけの仕返しをせよと説かれていますが、『新約』ではその箇所に言及し撤回しています。
　マルコムXは「イスラムの民」の広報代表格であった頃も教団から離れた後も、キング牧師らの「非暴力哲学」を「turn-the-other-cheek philosophy」とか「turn-the-other-cheekish」などと、聖書のことばを用いながら厳しく非難

します。

Spellman: What is your attitude toward Christian-Gandhian groups?
Malcolm: Christian? Gandhian? I don't go for anything that's nonviolent and turn-the-other-cheekish. I don't see how any revolution — I've never heard of a nonviolent revolution or a revolution that was brought about by turning the other cheek, and so I believe that it is a crime for anyone to teach a person who is being brutalized to continue to accept that brutality without doing something to defend himself. If this is what the Christian-Gandhian philosophy teaches, then it is criminal — a criminal philosophy.
(Breitman 1992: 8-9)

KKKなどからリンチを受け、家を焼かれ、教会を爆破され、抗議行動を起こせば警察に棍棒で殴られ、犬をけしかけられ、消火ホースの水で追い払われるといった残虐行為を受けている黒人に向かって、「無防備」、「無抵抗」を説くことは、「犯罪的」だと彼は言い、「自衛 (self-defense)」を主張します。

Concerning nonviolence: it is criminal to teach a man not to defend himself when he is the constant victim of brutal attacks. It is legal and lawful to own a shotgun or a rifle. We believe in obeying the law.

In areas where our people are the constant victims of brutality, and the government seems unable or unwilling to protect them, we should form rifle clubs that can be used to defend our lives and our property in times of emergency, such as happened last year in Birmingham; Plaquemine, Louisiana; Cambridge, Maryland; and Danville, Virginia. When our people are being bitten by dogs, they are within their rights to kill those dogs.

We should be peaceful, law-abiding — but the time has come for the American Negro to fight back in self-defense whenever and wherever he is being unjustly and unlawfully attacked.

If the government thinks I am wrong for saying this, then let the government start doing its jobs.

(Breitman 1992: 22)

当時の米国のマスコミは、マルコムXや「イスラムの民」を「暴力の唱道者」とか「戦闘的ムスリム」などと表現しましたが、「イスラムの民」も組織脱退後のマルコムXも、アフリカ系米国人に対して、武装して白人を正当な理由なく攻撃せよと扇動したことはありませんし、集会を除けばデモ行進などの抗議行動を起こしたこともほとんどなかったのです。脱退後のマルコムXも含めて、「イスラムの民」が主張していたのはあくまでも法律の範囲内での「自衛」でした。

彼らの「自衛」哲学を規定していたと思われるものは2つあり、1つが米国憲法、もう1つが『コーラン』の教えです。

AMENDMENT II

A well regulated Militia, being necessary to the security of a free State, the right of the people to keep and bear Arms, shall not be infringed.
(「よく統制された国民義勇軍は自由な国の安全保障にとって必要であるから、国民が武器を所有し、かつ携帯する権利は、これを侵害してはならない(飛田 1998: 167)」)

西暦1992年の日本人留学生射殺事件や、1999年の高校生の銃乱射殺害事件など、銃にかかわる事件が米国内で起こったときに必ず議論に出てくるのがこの米国憲法補正第2条(武器を所有し、携帯する権利条項)です。解釈をめぐって意見がさまざまに分かれ、所有できる武器の制限などは行われているようですが、現在でもこの条項自体は変わっていません。

当時マルコムXが「自衛は憲法で保証されている」というときに根拠としていたのはこの補正第2条でした。白人はあたりまえのようにライフルを所有し、ライフルクラブを作り、KKKのように武装して組織的暴力を行使する者も存在する。そのことは棚上げしながら、アフリカ系米国人がライフルやショットガンで武装して、不当な暴力から身を守れるような状態にしておくよう訴える

と白人中心のマスコミは彼を「暴力の扇動者」と呼んだのです。その欺瞞を指摘する際に彼はこの「武器を所有し、かつ携帯する権利条項」を用いました。

彼の、そして「イスラムの民」の「自衛」哲学のもう1つの拠り所がイスラムの啓典『コーラン』です。ちょっと余計なことですが、先に見たユダヤ教、キリスト教の啓典『聖書』も、そして『コーラン』も元々英語で書かれたわけではありません。それぞれ『聖書』はヘブライ語（『新約聖書』はギリシャ語）、『コーラン』はアラビア語で書かれました。いずれの聖典も原典でさえ様々な解釈がなされますから、翻訳するとますます内容がはっきり異なる箇所が多くなります。聖書の英訳でも版が異なれば別の解釈がなされることはすでに見たとおりです。次の『コーラン』の現代英語訳版からの引用も「1つの解釈」に過ぎません。マルコムXは英語版『コーラン』を読んだのは間違いないとしても、これとは異なる可能性が高いと思われます。それでも1つの参考にはなるでしょう。ついでながら、アラビア語の原典から直接日本語に訳されたものも付けました。

Al-Qur'ān 2 The Cow: 178, 179

178. O believers, ordained for you is retribution for the murdered, (whether) a free man (is guilty) of (the murder of) a free man, or a slave of a slave, or a woman of a woman. But he who is pardoned some of it by his brother should be dealt with equity, and recompense (for blood) paid with a grace. This is a concession from your Lord and a kindness. He who transgresses in spite of it shall suffer painful punishment.

179. In retribution there is life (and preservation). O men of sense, you may haply take heed for yourselves.

(Ali 1988: 32)

『コーラン』第2章　牝牛

　　（173[178]これ、信徒のものよ、殺人の場合には返報法（いわゆる「目には目、歯には歯を」）が規定であるぞ。つまり自由人には自由人、奴隷には奴隷、女には女（つまり1人に対して同格のもの1人の復讐である。1人殺されたのに、その復讐として相手側の人々をむやみに幾人も殺すというイスラム以前のならわしはもはや許さ

れない)。しかも(殺人を犯しても)、同胞(相手の当事者)が赦すと言った場合(復讐として犯人を殺すかわりに、いわゆる「血の価」── たとえば駱駝何頭の支払い ── で満足する場合)には、(復讐者の側では)正々堂々とことをはこばねばならないし、また(本人の方でも)立派な態度で償いの義務を果すのだ。174 これは神様が汝らに(報復の規律を)軽減して下さったのじゃ。つまり神様のお慈悲であるぞ。されば今後(この定め)を破るものがあれば、痛い神罰を蒙るであろうぞ。175[179]この返報法こそは汝らにとって生命(の源)となるもの(従来はこちらが1人殺されたら相手の部族の100人を殺せ式でやっていたからいたずらに生命の損失ばかり多かった。今度の新規定はアラブの復讐心を合理的に満足させ、しかも生命の喪失を最小限度にくいとめる)。よいか、汝らも物が分かるのだからな。(この定めを守るなら)きっと汝らも本当に神を畏れかしこむ者となるであろうぞ。)

(井筒 1964: 43)

「イスラム教」と聞くと、キリスト教をはじめとする他宗教を完全に排除してしまうような過激な印象を持たれている人も多いのかもしれませんが、実際には特にユダヤ教やキリスト教に対しては寛容であるようです。『コーラン』においてはマホメット(ムハンマド)が「最後の預言者」でありますが、彼以前に現れたモーセやイエスなども「預言者(神と同一ではない)」としては認められているのです。ただ、ユダヤ教徒、キリスト教徒などの「啓典の民」が自分たちの啓典(『聖書』)を誤って解釈したり使徒を神格化する過ちを犯したため、最後の使徒としてマホメットが神によって遣わされたと信じられているのです。ですから『コーラン』は『聖書』を否定するものではなく、むしろ確証するものであり、「本質的にその内容は普遍的なものである(中村 1998: 45)」とされます。

内容的に『コーラン』と『聖書』が似たような箇所を持つのはこのような背景によります。ここで取り上げた「同害報復刑」にしても、ユダヤ教の『聖書』にも出てきていることは先に見たとおりです。キリスト教の『新約聖書』では、それが否定され「もう片方の頬を向けよ」という教えになっている部分もあるわけですが、上で述べたとおり『コーラン』はムスリムにとっては、神から与えられた最後の啓典ですから、「同害報復」は普遍性を持つ教えとなります。

マルコムXはこの「同害報復」の教えを、公民権運動家たちの「非暴力」哲学を批判する文脈でしばしば使いました。しかし「正統派イスラム」でのそれは単に「何か危害を加えられたら仕返ししろ」という教えではありません。上の日本語の注釈にもあるように、「1人殺されたのに、その復讐として相手側の人々をむやみに幾人も殺すというイスラム以前のならわし」を制限し、刑をむしろ軽くする目的が本来その教えにはあったのです。またこの刑が実際行われるには多くの条件があるようです。

　報復が認められるのは、人が故意かつ不当に殺したり、傷害を加えたりした場合であるが、その場合でも条件がある。犯人が成人であること、知的に成熟していること、被害者が加害者と対等であること（奴隷と自由人、非ムスリムとムスリム、父と子の間では同害報復はありえない）である。

(中村 1998: 126-7)

厳密に言えば、米国内の白人はその多くがキリスト教徒すなわち非ムスリムですから、この刑罰は適用できません。マルコムXがこの教えを持ち出した理由は、何百年にもわたって虐げられてきたアフリカ系米国人の自然に持つ復讐心を満足させる1つの方便として用いたか、多くのキリスト教が知っている『旧約聖書』から持ち出したか、あるいは「イスラムの民」として、自分たちに合わせてそれを解釈し直したかのいずれかだと思われます。

　「イスラムの民」の「自衛」思想の根拠として『米国憲法とコーラン』を挙げましたが、もう1つこの思想を正当化する便法、「コミュニケーションのための言語」があります。これはおそらくマルコムX自身が作った「たとえ」だと思われます。

> I have to take time to mention that because, in my opinion, not only in Mississippi and Alabama, but right here in New York City, you and I can best learn how to get real freedom by studying how Kenyatta brought it to his people in Kenya, and how Odinga helped him, and the excellent job that was done by the Mau Mau freedom fighters. In fact, that's what we need in Mississippi. In Mississippi we need a Mau Mau. In Alabama we need a Mau Mau. In Georgia we need a Mau Mau. Right here in Harlem, in New

York City, we need a Mau Mau.

I say it with no anger; I say it with very careful forethought. The language that you and I have been speaking to this man in the past hasn't reached him. And you can never really get your point across to a person until you learn how to communicate with him. If he speaks French, you can't speak German. You have to know what language he speaks and then speak to him in that language.

(Breitman 1990: 106)

　歴史を考え、そして今自分たちの周りで生じている現実を見ると、米国白人の理解可能な「言語」は「暴力」という「言語」だと彼は言うのです。この「たとえ」の背景には、「言語」や「コミュニケーション」に対して彼が少なからぬ関心を持っていたことがあります。

　刑務所内で読んで感動した本の中に言語学の本があり、できることなら言語の研究もしてみたかったと彼は自伝で述べています。また「イスラムの民」を脱退後メッカ巡礼に行った際、英語しか分からない彼は「コミュニケーション」がまったくできない状況を経験します。その後自分でアラビア語の勉強を始めましたし、スワヒリ語や中国語なども勉強してみたかったようです。

　また、子供の頃には弁護士になりたいという「夢」(その夢を学校の教師に言うと、「もっと現実的に大工にでもなった方がよい。君はニガーなんだから」と一蹴されました)を持ち、後年にも自伝で「できるものなら弁護士になりたかった」と述べています。「自分ならいい弁護士になれたと思う」と。彼は人が理解できることばで話し、人を説得することが好きであり、得意であったのです。

　言語に関心を持ち、効果的なコミュニケーションの技術を持ち得た彼の、誰にでも伝わりその多くを納得させてしまうようなたとえの1つがこの「米国白人の暴力行為＝彼らの言語」だという気がします。

　以上のような根拠や「たとえ」で彼は「非暴力」を批判し、「自衛」を強調し続けたのです。もう一度言っておきますが、「自衛」であって「暴力」でも「仕返し」でもありません。もっともこの点については、キング牧師の次の指摘も一考に値します。

... it is extremely dangerous to organize a movement around self-defense. The line between defensive violence and aggressive or retaliatory violence is a fine line indeed. When violence is tolerated even as a means of self-defense there is grave danger that in the fervor of emotion the main fight will be lost over the question of self-defense.

(Washington 1992: 130)

「自衛」のための暴力と「攻撃ないしは報復」のための暴力は紙一重だというわけです。マルコムXの「自衛」のための武装は多分に白人権力や白人至上主義に対する威嚇の意味が含まれているとはいえ、相手が武器を使えばこちらも武器を使うという論理になり、現実に黒人対白人の戦争に発展すれば人口や武装規模の差は歴然としており、米国黒人に勝ち目はないでしょう。ある意味で、米国黒人神学者のジェイムス・H・コーン氏も言うように、「非暴力」こそがアフリカ系米国人が解放闘争の際とり得た唯一最適の方法であったのかもしれません。現に無防備の黒人の抗議行動に対して、犬をけしかけたり消火栓の水をかけたりする警察の残虐行為がマスコミによって米国内だけでなく海外にも流れ、世論に訴えることが可能となったのも事実です。「非暴力」哲学が、キング牧師のねらいどおり、キリスト教に規定される白人の道徳心や良心に訴え、一定の成功をおさめた側面も見逃してはならないでしょう。

マルコムXが西暦1965年に凶弾に倒れ39歳の人生を終えたとき、「暴力」を唱えたために殺されたと「イスラムの民」のイライジャ・ムハマドは言っています。キング牧師が「夢」演説をしたあの「平和大行進」の後の公民権法、投票権法の制定にもかかわらず次々と起こった下層階級のアフリカ系米国人暴動に対して、マルコムXは暴動を起こした当事者たちを弁護しました。当時ベトナム戦争のさなかということもあり、「米国が国外では暴力を行使しておきながら国内の黒人だけに「非暴力」を要求することはできない」と。確かに、彼が「暴力」を扇動したと見る人もいて不思議はないかもしれません。

しかし、黒人の暴動に対して常に「非暴力」を訴え続けていたあのキング牧師でさえ晩年には次のように述べています。

... As I have walked among the desperate, rejected, and angry young men, I have told them that Molotov cocktails and rifles would not solve their problems. I have tried to offer them my deepest compassion while maintaining my conviction that social change comes most meaningfully through nonviolent action. But they asked, and rightly so, "What about Vietnam?" They asked if our own nation wasn't using massive doses of violence to solve its problems, to bring about the changes it wanted. Their questions hit home, and I knew that I could never again raise my voice against the violence of the oppressed in the ghettos without having first spoken clearly to the greatest purveyor of violence in the world today: my own government. For the sake of those boys, for the sake of this government, for the sake of the hundreds of thousands trembling under our violence, I cannot be silent.
("Beyond Vietnam" (1967) スピーチ (http://www.stanford.edu/group/king/speeches/Beyond_Vietnam.htm) より)

　マルコムXのことばと酷似した内容となっています。暴動を起こす黒人に向かうよりも、国に向かって非難の声をあげる方が先だと言うのです。公民権運動団体にとって、ベトナムに関する政策批判は国を完全に敵に回してしまうことになり「口にしてはならないこと」であったのですが、キング牧師は国家の「暴力」を批判せずして国内で暴力に訴える黒人に「非暴力」を説くことはできなかったのです。もちろんあくまでも「非暴力を貫け」という結論に変化はないのですが、暴力批判の矛先をアフリカ系米国人から国家に向け、ついに白人米国政府に敵対する立場に立ってしまった彼は、この演説の翌年狙撃されマルコムXと同じ39歳で亡くなります。
　「自衛」を唱えたマルコムXも「非暴力」を唱えたキング牧師も同様に「暴力」の犠牲となったのです。

● 人権 (human rights)

公民権運動（Civil Rights Movement）はその名のとおり「公民権」を米国政府に要求する運動でした。マルコムXは、特に「イスラムの民」脱退後、アフリカ系米国人の闘争目標を「公民権」要求から「人権」要求の水準に引き上げることを強く主張し始めます。世界中で抑圧、搾取されている多くの非白人と連帯を図り、ある意味で「世界政府」的役割を持つと考えられている国際連合に訴えかけることを彼は目論んだのです。白人に黒人の扱い方を変えるよう国内で訴えるよりも、「外圧」をかける方が効果的だというわけです。

When we begin to get in this area, we need new friends, we need new allies. We need to expand the civil-rights struggle to a higher level — to the level of human rights. Whenever you are in a civil-rights struggle, whether you know it or not, you are confining yourself to the jurisdiction of Uncle Sam. No one from the outside world can speak out in your behalf as long as your struggle is a civil-rights struggle. Civil rights comes within the domestic affairs of this country. All of our African brothers and our Asian brothers and our Latin-American brothers cannot open their mouths and interfere in the domestic affairs of the United States. And as long as it's civil rights, this comes under the jurisdiction of Uncle Sam.

But the United Nations has what's known as the charter of human rights, it has a committee that deals in human rights. You may wonder why all of the atrocities that have been committed in Africa and in Hungary and in Asia and in Latin America are brought before the UN, and the Negro problem is never brought before the UN. This is part of the conspiracy. This old, tricky, blue-eyed liberal who is supposed to be your and my friend, supposed to be in our corner, supposed to be subsidizing our struggle, and supposed to be acting in the capacity of an adviser, never tells you anything about human rights. They keep you wrapped up in civil-rights. And you spend so much time barking up the civil-rights tree, you don't even know there's a human-rights tree on the same floor.

When you expand the civil-rights struggle to the level of human-rights, you can then take the case of the black man in this country before the nations in the UN. You can take it before the General Assembly. You can take Uncle Sam before a world court. But the only level you can do it on is the level of human rights. Civil rights keeps you under his restrictions, under his jurisdiction. Civil rights keeps you in his pocket. Civil rights means you're asking Uncle Sam to treat you right. Human rights are something you were born with. Human rights are your God-given rights. Human rights are the rights that are recognized by all nations of this earth. And any time any one violates your human rights, you can take them to the world court. Uncle Sam's hands are dripping with blood, dripping with the blood of the black man in this country. He's the earth's number-one hypocrite. He has the audacity — yes, he has — imagine him posing as the leader of the free world. The free world! — and you over here singing "We Shall Overcome." Expand the civil-rights struggle to the level of human rights, take it into the United Nations, where our African brothers can throw their weight on our side, where our Asian brothers can throw their weight on our side, where our Latin-American brothers can throw their weight on our side, and where 800 million Chinaman are sitting there waiting to throw their weight on our side.

(Breitman 1990: 34-5)

ここでは、「公民権 (civil rights)」と「人権 (human rights)」との違いについて考える必要があります。まず「公民権」の辞書的定義から見てみましょう。

英語の「civil rights」は、『リーダーズ英和辞典』(1997) では、「市民権, 公民権; ＊《特に 黒人など少数民族グループの》平等権」と定義されています。「civil rights movement」は日本語では「公民権運動」と普通訳されるのですが、「公民権」は「市民権」や「平等権」と違うのでしょうか。それぞれ『広辞苑』

(第5版)の定義です。

市民権　①市民としての権利。人権・民権・公権とも同義に用いる。
　　　　②市民としての行動・思想・財産の自由が保障され、居住する地域・国家の政治に参加することのできる権利。

公民権　公民としての権利。国会または地方公共団体の議会や長に関する選挙権・被選挙権を通じて政治に参与する地位・資格などを指す。

平等権　国政において、人種・信条・性別・社会的身分・門地などにより差別されない権利。日本では憲法第14条で保障する。

それぞれ微妙に異なるようですが、一般的には「公民権」は国家や国政の範囲内での権利を示していることは何となく分かります。これを米国内での定義に限定すると次のようになります。

civil rights　　The rights belonging to an individual by virtue of citizenship, especially the fundamental freedoms and privileges guaranteed by the 13th and 14th Amendments to the U.S. Constitution and by subsequent acts of Congress, including civil liberties, due process, equal protection of the laws, and freedom from discrimination.　　(*American Heritage*, 3rd edition)

「合衆国憲法補正第13、14条」が出てきますから、それらもついでに見ておきましょう。それぞれ第1節のみを挙げました。

AMENDMENT XIII

Section 1. Neither slavery nor involuntary servitude, except as a punishment for crime whereof the party shall have been duly convicted, shall exist within the United States, or any place subject to their jurisdiction.

AMENDMENT XIV

Section 1. All persons born or naturalized in the United States, and subject to the jurisdiction thereof, are citizens of the United States and of the State wherein they reside. No State shall make or enforce any law which shall abridge the privileges or immunities of citizens of the United States; nor shall any State deprive any person of life, liberty, or property, without due process of law; nor deny to any person within its jurisdiction the equal protection of the laws.

簡単にいうと、第13条が「奴隷制度と強制労働の禁止」、14条が「奴隷制廃止に伴う市民権の拡大、法による平等な保護、適正な法手続など」に関する法律です（飛田 1998: 193-207参照）。
　米国における「公民権」とは、要するに米国の法律、特にこの補正13、14条で個々人に保障された米国民としての諸権利と言えます。
　次に「人権」ですが、これも辞書（『広辞苑』と American Heritage）の定義から始めます。

人権　（human rights）　人間が人間として生れながらに持っている権利。実定法上の権利のように自由に剥奪または制限されない。基本的人権。

human rights　The basic rights and freedoms to which all human beings are entitled, often held to include the right to life and liberty, freedom of thought and expression, and equality before the law.

　「生まれながらに持っている」と「entitled（資格や権利を与えられた）」とは微妙に異なります。「持っている」は人間が主体ですが、「entitled」はそれを与える誰か（何か）が必要になります。一体誰（何）に与えられたのでしょうか？　この英語の定義を見る限り、人間や法律よりも優先される「誰か（何か）」の存在を前提としているとしか言えません。マルコムXの上の演説をよく読めばその「何か」は「神」であることが分かります。また先に引用した『独立宣言』を読んでも同じことが言えます。ここで再び、今度は少し長めに引用します。

When in the Course of human events, it becomes necessary for one people to dissolve the political bands which have connected them with another, and to assume, among the Powers of the earth, the separate and equal station to which the Laws of Nature and of Nature's God entitle them, a decent respect to the opinions of mankind requires that they should declare the causes which impel them to the separation.

We hold these truths to be self-evident, that all men are created equal, that they are endowed by their Creator with certain unalienable Rights, that among these are Life, Liberty, and the pursuit of Happiness. That to secure these rights, Governments are instituted among Men, deriving their just powers from the consent of the governed, That whenever any Form of Government becomes destructive of these ends, it is the Right of the People to alter or to abolish it, and to institute new Government, laying its foundation on such principles and organizing its powers in such form, as to them shall seem most likely to effect their Safety and Happiness. ...

　この『独立宣言』は米国建国の理念ですから、米国民の大部分が「人権」は「神」に賦与されたという信念を共有していると言ってよいと思われます。侵すことのできない「生命、自由および幸福追求の権利」を与える存在とは、「創造主 (Creator)」すなわち「神 (God)」であり、これらの権利を守るために人間によって政府というものが作られたのであるから、その目的を果たせない場合は政府を廃止して作り直してもよいのです。

　ここで「公民権」と「人権」との違いがはっきり分かります。国家、政府そして法律を作るのは人間です。その人間を作ったのは神であり、神は人間を完全に超越する存在である以上、神が与えた権利（人権）は「絶対」であり、国家の法律など（人間）が保障する権利（公民権）に優先されるどころか、人間がそれを「侵すことなどできない」のです。

　ただ、独立宣言の「神」は基本的に「キリスト教の神」、マルコムXの神は「イスラム教の神（アラー）」という違いは確かにあります。しかし、イスラム教徒もキリスト教徒も唯一神を信じる点では共通です。いずれにとっても「人

権」が「神」によって与えられたことを認めるなら、それが「人間」によって作られた「公民権」に優先されるということはあたりまえのことなのです。米国の白人もキリスト教徒が多数派ですから「人権」を否定することなどできません。

「公民権」と「人権」は以上のような違いがあり、一神教信者の国家（共同体）では「人権」が「公民権」よりも優先されるという共通認識があることがはっきりしましたが、マルコムXはこの共通認識をさらに一歩進めて、「人権は世界のすべての国家に認められている」とします。そして「米国内の公民権問題」ではなく「世界の西半球にある一地域での人権問題」として、アフリカ系米国人の問題を「世界」すなわち「国連」に提示することを主張したのです。「権力」にはより大きな「権力」で、という考え方です。

あらゆる政治行動に直接関与することを禁じていた「イスラムの民」の制約から解放された彼は、「人権」の概念を米国の聴衆にただ訴えただけでなく実際に行動も起こしました。1964年「イスラムの民」脱退直後、マルコムXは立て続けに「ムスリム・モスク（Muslim Mosque, Inc.）」という名の新宗教組織、さらに「アフロ・アメリカン統一機構（OAAU）」と称する、宗教とは無関係の新組織を結成しました。同じ年彼は「OAAU」代表として、独立したアフリカ諸国が1963年に結成した国際機構である「アフリカ統一機構（OAU）」の第2回会議にオブザーバーとして出席を許され、各国代表にメモランダムを提出しました。その内容は、米国の黒人に関する人権問題を各国首脳に提示し、国連人権委員会への即時調査勧告を彼らに依頼するものでした。

結果として、米国の「人権」問題に関する提訴は1964年の国連会議ではなされなかったものの、アフリカ系米国人とアフリカとの連帯を様々な意味で実現し、国連全体はもとより、特にその機関内の人権擁護の面で指導的立場にある米国政府に大きな警戒心を持たせたことは事実であったようです。

帰国後彼は「OAAU」を基盤とし、以前批判していた公民権運動団体に謝罪すると同時に、人権概念を基軸に連帯を呼びかけます。しかし、最後まで「自衛」思想を持ち続けたこともあり、公民権運動との連携は実現しませんでした。

●「あるがまま」のマルコム X 演説

　以上、マルコム X の思想の中心概念である「黒人民族主義」、彼の闘争の基本方針である「自衛」、米国黒人問題の解決策として彼が最終的に到達した概念「人権」に焦点をあて、その意図、根拠あるいは意義を解釈、考察しました。特に同時代の代表的な公民権運動家であるキング牧師との比較も適宜試みながら、マルコム X の思想の基本的な部分が、ある程度「明らめ」られるよう心がけたつもりです。

　しかしながら、人のことばを部分的に引用して解説を加える作業では、短時間でその概要を知るのには有効とはいえ、「使われたことば」がその文脈でのみ持つ重要な側面を見落としたり、発話者の意図とは異なる不適切な解釈をしてしまうこともあります。人の発言を一部あるいは一語だけとりあげて大騒ぎし、それが単なる揚げ足取りに終わってしまうことなどはその典型的な例です。たとえば、いわゆる「差別語」などと呼ばれることばも、その文脈、すなわち、誰が、誰に対して、いつ、どこで、どのような前後関係で使われたかによって、「差別語」でなくなることもあれば、逆に「差別語」でなくとも、文脈によっては「差別語」となってしまうこともあるのです。いわゆる「差別語」だけではありません。どのような語であっても、より的確に意図をくみ取ろうと思えば、多くの場合、より長い文脈が必要となります。

　そこで本章後半では、マルコム X の意図をより適切に理解していただくため、部分的に引用して解説を加えるのではなく、彼の演説をできるだけ「あるがまま」の形で紹介したいと思います。もちろん彼が行った数多くの演説のすべてを示すことはできませんから、入手可能な代表的演説の中から 2 つのみ引用します。ただし、この 2 つの演説でさえ実は完全原稿ではありません。彼自身の希望で後に削除された部分も少なからずありますし、本書の頁の都合上、割愛せざるを得ない部分もあります。それでも、かなりまとまった量の原稿を見ていただくことにより、彼の思想に対する理解が少なくとも現時点よりは深いものになると期待できます。それぞれの演説の背景情報となる最低限の解説のみ付けますから、これまでで得られた知識を前提に、演説が行われている場面を

想像しながら、あるいは可能であればマルコムXの視点に立つことを試みながら読んでみて下さい。

●「黒人大衆へのメッセージ」

1つ目は、1963年11月9日と10日にデトロイトで行われた「黒人大衆へのメッセージ（Message to the Grass Roots）」と呼ばれる演説です。マルコムXは、進歩的指導者グループの協力者であるアルバート・B・クリーグ・ジュニア牧師主催の北部下層黒人指導者会議に出席し、そのクライマックスとも呼べる大規模な大衆集会の主な演説者の1人としてこの演説を行いました。このころの彼はまだ「イスラムの民」の教団員でしたから、この演説はイライジャ・ムハマドの代弁者としてなされたものと言えます。聴衆の大部分は黒人ですが、集会の性質（キリスト教牧師主催）上「イスラムの民」の教団員ではありません。

この演説には、「黒人民族主義」に関する彼の考えや、キング牧師ら公民権運動家たちの姿勢や方法に対する見方がよく表れています。特にキング牧師の「I Have a Dream」演説を含む同年8月のワシントン大行進についても彼は言及し、「大成功」と評価された行進に対する別の視点を提供します。

And during the few moments that we have left we want to have just an off-the-cuff chat between you and me, us. We want to talk right down to earth in a language that everybody here can easily understand. We all agree tonight, all of the speakers have agreed, that America has a very serious problem. Not only does America have a very serious problem, but our people have a very serious problem. America's problem is us. We're her problem. The only reason she has a problem is she doesn't want us here. And every time you look at yourself, be you black, brown, red or yellow, a so-called Negro, you represent a person who poses such a serious problem for America because you're not wanted. Once you face this as a fact, then you can start plotting a course that will make you appear intelligent, instead of unintelligent.

What you and I need to do is learn to forget our differences. When we come together, we don't come together as Baptists or Methodists. You don't catch hell because you're a Baptist, and you don't catch hell because you're a Methodist. You don't catch hell because you're a Methodist or Baptist, you don't catch hell because you're a Democrat or a Republican, you don't catch hell because you're a Mason or an Elk, and you sure don't catch hell because you're an American; because if you were an American, you wouldn't catch hell. You catch hell because you're a black man. You catch hell, all of us catch hell, for the same reason.

So we're all black people, so-called Negroes, second-class citizens, ex-slaves. You're nothing but an ex-slave. You don't like to be told that. But what else are you? You are ex-slaves. You didn't come here on the "Mayflower." You came here on a slave ship. In chains, like a horse, or a cow, or a chicken. And you were brought here by the people who came here on the "Mayflower," you were brought here by the so-called Pilgrims, or Founding Fathers. They were the ones who brought you here.

We have a common enemy. We have this in common: We have a common oppressor, a common exploiter, and a common discriminator. But once we all realize that we have the common enemy, then we unite — on the basis of what we have in common. And what we have foremost in common is that enemy — the white man. He's an enemy to all of us. I know some of you all think that some of them aren't enemies. Time will tell.

In Bandung back in, I think, 1954, was the first unity meeting in centuries of black people. And once you study what happened at the Bandung conference, and the results of the Bandung conference, it actually serves as a model for the same procedure you and I can use to get our problems solved. At Bandung all the nations came together, (they were) the dark nations from Africa and Asia. Some of them were Buddhists, some of them were Muslims, some of them were Christians, some were Confucianists, some were atheists.

Despite their religious differences, they came together. Some were communists, some were socialists, some were capitalists — despite their economic and political differences, they came together. All of them were black, brown, red or yellow.

The number-one thing that was not allowed to attend the Bandung conference was the white man. He couldn't come. Once they excluded the white man, they found that they could get together. Once they kept him out, everybody else fell right in and fell in line. This is the thing that you and I have to understand. And these people who came together didn't have nuclear weapons, they didn't have jet planes, they didn't have all of the heavy armaments that the white man has. But they had unity.

They were able to submerge their little petty differences and agree on one thing: That there one African came from Kenya and was being colonized by the Englishman, and another African came from the Congo and was being colonized by the Belgian, and another African came from Guinea and was being colonized by the French, and another came from Angola and was being colonized by the Portuguese. When they came to the Bandung conference, they looked at the Portuguese, and at the Frenchman, and at the Englishman, and at the Dutchman, and learned or realized the one thing that all of them had in common — they were all from Europe, they were all Europeans, blond, blue-eyed and white skins. They began to recognize who their enemy was. The same man that was colonizing our people in Kenya was colonizing our people in the Congo. The same one in the Congo was colonizing our people in South Africa, and in Southern Rhodesia, and in Burma, and in India, and in Afghanistan, and in Pakistan. They realized all over the world where the dark man was being oppressed, he was being oppressed by the white man; where the dark man was being exploited, he was being exploited by the white man. So they got together on this basis — that they had a common enemy.

And when you and I here in Detroit and in Michigan and in America who have been awakened today look around us, we too realize here in America we all have a common enemy, whether he's in Georgia or Michigan, whether he's in California or New York. He's the same man — blue eyes and blond hair and pale skin — the same man. So what we have to do is what they did. They agreed to stop quarreling among themselves. Any little spat that they had, they'd settle it among themselves, go into a huddle — don't let the enemy know that you've got a disagreement.

Instead of airing our differences in public, we have to realize we're all the same family. And when you have a family squabble, you don't get out on the sidewalk. If you do, everybody calls you uncouth, unrefined, uncivilized, savage. If you don't make it at home, you settle it at home; you get in the closet, argue it out behind closed doors, and then when you come out on the street, you pose a common front, a united front. And this is what we need to do in the community, and in the city, and in the state. We need to stop airing our differences in front of the white man, put the white man out of our meeting, and then sit down and talk shop with each other. That's what we've got to do.

I would like to make a few comments concerning the differences between the black revolution and the Negro revolution. There's a difference. Are they both the same? And if they're not, what is the difference? What is the difference between a black revolution and a Negro revolution? First, what is a revolution? Sometimes I'm inclined to believe that many of our people are using this word "revolution" loosely, without taking careful consideration of what this word actually means, and what its historic characteristics are. When you study the historic nature of revolutions, the motive of a revolution, the objective of a revolution, the result of a revolution, and the methods used in a revolution, you may change words. You may devise another program, you may change your goal and you may change your mind.

Look at the American Revolution in 1776. That revolution was for what? For land. Why did they want land? Independence. How was it carried out? Bloodshed. Number one, it was based on land, the basis of independence.

And the only way they could get it was bloodshed. The French Revolution — what was it based on? The landless against the landlord. What was it for? Land. How did they get it? Bloodshed. Was no love lost, was no compromise, was no negotiation. I'm telling you — you don't know what a revolution is. Because when you find out what it is, you'll get back in the alley, you'll get out of the way.

The Russian Revolution — what was it based on? Land; the landless against the landlord. How did they bring it about? Bloodshed. You haven't got a revolution that doesn't involve bloodshed. And you're afraid to bleed. I said, you're afraid to bleed.

As long as the white man sent you to Korea, you bled. He sent you to Germany, you bled. He sent you to the South Pacific to fight the Japanese, you bled. You bleed for white people, but when it comes to seeing your own churches being bombed and little black girls murdered, you haven't got any blood. You bleed when the white man says bleed; you bite when the white man says bite; and you bark when the white man says bark. I hate to say this about us, but it's true. How are you going to be nonviolent in Mississippi, as violent as you were in Korea? How can you justify being nonviolent in Mississippi and Alabama, when your churches are being bombed, and your little girls are being murdered, and at the same time you are going to get violent with Hitler, and Tojo, and somebody else you don't even know?

If violence is wrong in America, violence is wrong abroad. If it is wrong to be violent defending black women and black children and black babies and black men, then it is wrong for America to draft us and make us violent abroad in defense of her. And if it is right for America to draft us, and teach us how to be violent in defense of her, then it is right for you and me to do whatever is necessary to defend our own people right here in this country.

The Chinese Revolution — they wanted land. They threw the British out, along with the Uncle Tom Chinese. Yes, they did. They set a good example. When I was in prison, I read an article — don't be shocked when I say that I was in prison. You're still in prison. That's what America means: prison. When I was in prison, I read an article in *Life* magazine showing a little Chinese girl, nine years old; her father was on his hands and knees and she was pulling the trigger because he was an Uncle Tom Chinaman. When they had the revolution over there, they took a whole generation of Uncle Toms and just wiped them out. And within ten years that little girl became a full-grown woman. No more Toms in China. And today it's one of the toughest, roughest, most feared countries on this earth — by the white man. Because there are no Uncle Toms over there.

Of all our studies, history is best qualified to reward our research. And when you see that you've got problems, all you have to do is examine the historic method used all over the world by others who have problems similar to yours. Once you see how they got theirs straight, then you know how you can get yours straight. There's been a revolution, a black revolution, going on in Africa. In Kenya, the Mau Mau were revolutionary; they were the ones who brought the word "Uhuru" to the fore. The Mau Mau, they were revolutionary, they believed in scorched earth, they knocked everything aside that got in their way, and their revolution also was based on land, a desire for land. In Algeria, the northern part of Africa, a revolution took place. The Algerians were revolutionists, they wanted land. France offered to let them be integrated into France. They told France, to hell with France, they wanted some land, not some France. And they engaged in a bloody battle.

So I cite these various revolutions, brothers and sisters, to show you that you don't have a peaceful revolution. You don't have a turn-the-other-cheek revolution. There's no such thing as a nonviolent revolution. The only kind of revolution that is nonviolent is the Negro revolution. The only revolution in which the goal is loving your enemy is the Negro revolution. It's the only revolution in which the goal is a desegregated lunch counter, a desegregated theater, a desegregated park, and a desegregated pubic toilets; you can sit down next to white folks — on the toilets. That's no revolution. Revolution is based on land. Land is the basis of all independence. Land is the basis of freedom, justice, and equality.

The white man knows what a revolution is. He knows that the black revolution is world-wide in scope and in nature. The black revolution is sweeping Asia, is sweeping Africa, is rearing its head in Latin America. The Cuban Revolution — that's a revolution. They overturned the system. Revolution is in Asia, revolution is in Africa, and the white man is screaming because he sees revolution in Latin America. How do you think he'll react to you when you learn what a real revolution is? You don't know what a revolution is. If you did, you wouldn't use that word.

Revolution is bloody, revolution is hostile, revolution knows no compromise, revolution overturns and destroys everything that gets in its way. And you, sitting around here like a knot on the wall, saying, "I'm going to love these folks no matter how much they hate me." No, you need a revolution. Whoever heard of a revolution where they lock arms, as Rev. Cleage was pointing out beautifully, singing "We Shall Overcome"? You don't do that in a revolution. You don't do any singing, you're too busy swinging. It's based on land. A revolutionary wants land so he can set up his own nation, an independent nation. These Negroes aren't asking for any nation — they're trying to crawl back on the plantation.

When you want a nation, that's called nationalism. When the white man became involved in a revolution in this country against England, what was it for? He wanted this land so he could set up another white nation. That's white nationalism. The American Revolution was white nationalism. The French Revolution was white nationalism. The Russian Revolution too — yes, it was — white nationalism. You don't think so? Why do you think Khrushchev and Mao can't get their heads together? White nationalism. All the revolutions that are going on in Asia and Africa today are based on what? — black nationalism. A revolutionary is a black nationalist. He wants a nation. I was reading some beautiful words by Rev. Cleage, pointing out why he couldn't get together with someone else in the city because all of them were afraid of being identified with black nationalism. If you're afraid of black nationalism, you're afraid of revolution. And if you love revolution, you love black nationalism.

To understand this, you have to go back to what the young brother here referred to as the house Negro and the field Negro back during slavery. There were two kinds of slaves, the house Negro and the field Negro. The house Negroes — they lived in the house with master, they dressed pretty good, they ate good because they ate his food — what he left. They lived in the attic or the basement, but still they lived near the master; and they loved the master more than the master loved himself. They would give their life to save the master's house — quicker than the master would. If the master said, "We got a good house here," the house Negro would say, "Yeah, we got a good house here." Whenever the master said "we," he said "we." That's how you can tell a house Negro.

If the master's house caught on fire, the house Negro would fight harder to put the blaze out than the master would. If the master got sick, the house Negro would say, "What's the matter, boss, *we* sick?" *We* sick! He identified himself with his master, more than his master identified with himself. And if you came to the house Negro and said, "Let's run away, let's escape, let's separate," the house Negro would look at you and say, "Man, you crazy. What you mean, separate? Where is there a better house than this? Where can I wear better clothes than this? Where can I eat better food than this?" That was that house Negro. In those days he was called a "house nigger." And that's what we call them today, because we've still got some house niggers running around here.

This modern house Negro loves his master. He wants to live near him. He'll pay three times as much as the house is worth just to live near his master, and then brag about "I'm the only Negro out here." "I'm the only one on my job." "I'm the only one in this school." You're nothing but a house

Negro. And if someone comes to you right now and says, "Let's separate," you say the same thing that the house Negro said on the plantation. "What you mean, separate? From America, this good white man? Where you going to get a better job than you get here?" I mean, this is what you say. "I ain't left nothing in Africa," that's what you say. Why, you left your mind in Africa.

On that same plantation, there was the field Negro. The field Negroes — those were the masses. There were always more Negroes in the field than there were Negroes in the house. The Negro in the field caught hell. He ate leftovers. In the house they ate high up on the hog. The Negro in the field didn't get anything but what was left of the insides of the hog. They call it "chitt'lings" nowadays. In those days they called them what they were — guts. That's what you were — gut-eaters. And some of you are still gut-eaters.

The field Negro was beaten from morning to night; he lived in a shack, in a hut; he wore old, castoff clothes. He hated his master. I say he hated his master. He was intelligent. That house Negro loved his master, but that field Negro — remember, they were in the majority, and they hated the master. When the house caught on fire, he didn't try to put it out; that field Negro prayed for a wind, for a breeze. When the master got sick, the field Negro prayed that he'd die. If someone came to the field Negro and said, "Let's separate, let's run," he didn't say "Where we going?" He'd say, "Any place is better than here." You've got field Negroes in America today. I'm a field Negro. The masses are the field Negroes. When they see this man's house on fire, you don't hear the little Negroes talking about "*our* government is in trouble." They say, "*The* government is in trouble." Imagine a Negro: "*Our* government"! I even heard one say "*our* astronauts." They won't even let him near the plant — and "*our* astronauts"! "*Our* Navy" — that's a Negro that is out of his mind, a Negro that is out of his mind.

Just as the slavemaster of that day used Tom, the house Negro, to keep the field Negroes in check, the same old slavemaster today has Negroes who are nothing but modern Uncle Toms, twentieth-century Uncle Toms, to keep you and me in check, to keep us under control, keep us passive and peaceful and nonviolent. That's Tom making you nonviolent. It's like when you go to the dentist, and the man's going to take your tooth. You're going to fight him when he starts pulling. So he squirts some stuff in your jaw called novocaine, to make you think they're not doing anything to you. So you sit there and because you've got all of that novocaine in your jaw, you suffer — peacefully. Blood running all down your jaw, and you don't know what's happening. Because someone has taught you to suffer — peacefully.

The white man does the same thing to you in the street, when he wants to put knots on your head and take advantage of you and not have to be afraid of your fighting back. To keep you from fighting back, he gets these old religious Uncle Toms to teach you and me, just like novocaine, to suffer peacefully. Don't stop suffering — just suffer peacefully. As Rev. Cleage pointed out, they say you should let your blood flow in the streets. This is a shame. You know he's a Christian preacher. If it's a shame to him, you know what it is to me.

There is nothing in our book, the Koran, that teaches us to suffer peacefully. Our religion teaches us to be intelligent. Be peaceful, be courteous, obey the law, respect everyone; but if someone puts his hand on you, send him to the cemetery. That's a good religion. In fact, that's that old-time religion. That's the one that Ma and Pa used to talk about: an eye for an eye, and a tooth for a tooth, and a head for a head, and a life for a life. That's a good religion. And nobody resents that kind of religion being taught but a wolf, who intends to make you his meal.

This is the way it is with the white man in America. He's a wolf — and you're sheep. Any time a shepherd, a pastor, teaches you and me not to run from the white man and, at the same time, teaches us not to fight the white man, he's a traitor to you and me. Don't lay down a life all by itself. No, preserve your life, it's the best thing you've got. And if you've got to give it up, let it be even-steven. The slavemaster took Tom and dressed him well, fed him well and even gave him a little education — a *little* education; gave him a long coat and a top hat and made all the other slaves look up to him. Then he used Tom to control them. The same strategy that was used in those days is used today, by the same white man. He takes a Negro, a so-called Negro, and makes him prominent, builds him up, publicizes him, makes him a celebrity. And then he becomes a spokesman for Negroes — and a Negro leader.

I would like to mention just one other thing quickly, and that is the method that the white man uses, how the white man uses the "big guns," or Negro leaders, against the black revolution. They are not a part of the black revolution. They are used against the black revolution.

When Martin Luther King failed to desegregate Albany, Georgia, the civil-rights struggle in America reached its low point. King became bankrupt almost, as a leader. The Southern Christian Leadership Conference was in financial trouble; and it was in trouble, period, with the people when they failed to desegregate Albany, Georgia. Other Negro civil-rights leaders of so-called national stature became fallen idols. As they became fallen idols, began to lose their prestige and influence, local Negro leaders began to stir up the masses. In Cambridge, Maryland, Gloria Richardson; in Danville, Virginia, and other parts of the country, local leaders began to stir up our people at the grass-roots level. This was never done by these Negroes of national stature. They control you, but they have never incited you or excited you. They control you, they contain you, they have kept you on the plantation.

As soon as King failed in Birmingham, Negroes took to the streets. King went out to California to a big rally and raised I don't know how many thousands of dollars. He came to Detroit and had a march and raised some more thousands of dollars. And recall, right after that Roy Wilkins attacked King. He accused King and CORE [Congress Of Racial Equality] of starting trouble everywhere and then making the NAACP [National Association for the Advancement of Colored People] get them out of jail and spend a lot of money; they accused King and CORE of raising all the money and not paying it back. This happened; I've got it in documented evidence in the newspaper. Roy started attacking King, and King started attacking Roy, and Farmer started attacking both of them. And as these Negroes of national stature began to attack each other, they began to lose their control of the Negro masses.

The Negroes were out there in the streets. They were talking about how they were going to march on Washington. Right at that time Birmingham had exploded, and the Negroes in Birmingham — remember, they also exploded. They began to stab the crackers in the back and bust them up 'side their head — yes, they did. That's when Kennedy sent in the troops, down in Birmingham. After that, Kennedy got on the television and said "this is a moral issue." That's when he said he was going to put out a civil-rights bill. And when he mentioned civil-rights bill and the Southern crackers started talking about how they were going to boycott or filibuster it, then the Negroes started talking — about what? That they were going to march on Washington, march on the Senate, march on the White House, march on the Congress, and tie it up, bring it to a halt, not let the government proceed. They even said they were going out to the airport and lay down on the runway and not let any airplanes land. I'm telling you what they said. That was revolution. That was revolution. That was the black revolution.

It was the grass roots out there in the street. It scared the white man to death, scared the white power structure in Washington, D.C., to death; I was there. When they found out that this black steamroller was going to come down on the capital, they called in Wilkins, they called in Randolph, they called in these national Negro leaders that you respect and told them, "Call it off." Kennedy said, "Look, you all are letting this thing go too far." And Old Tom said, "Boss, I can't stop it, because I didn't start it." I'm telling you what they said. They said, "I'm not even in it, much less at the head of it." They said, "These Negroes are doing things on their own. They're running ahead of us." And that old shrewd fox, he said, "If you all aren't in it, I'll put you in it. I'll put you at the head of it. I'll endorse it. I'll welcome it. I'll help it. I'll join it."

A matter of hours went by. They had a meeting at the Carlyle Hotel in New York City. The Carlyle Hotel is owned by the Kennedy family; that's the hotel Kennedy spent the night at, two nights ago; it belongs to his family. A philanthropic society headed by a white man named Stephen Currier called all the top civil-rights leaders together at the Carlyle Hotel. And he told them, "By you all fighting each other, you are destroying the civil-rights movement. And since you're fighting over money from white liberals, let us set up what is known as the Council for United Civil Rights Leadership. Let's form this council, and all the civil-rights organizations will belong to it, and we'll use it for fund-raising purposes." Let me show you how tricky the white man is. As soon as they got it formed, they elected Whitney Young as its chairman, and who do you think became the co-chairman? Stephen Currier, the white man, a millionaire. Powell was talking about it down at Cobo Hall today. This is what he was talking about. Powell knows it happened. Randolph knows it happened. Wilkins knows it happened. King knows it happened. Every one of that Big Six — they know it happened.

Once they formed it, with the white man over it, he promised them and gave them $800,000 to split up among the Big Six; and told them that after the march was over they'd give them $700,000 more. A million and a half dollars — split up between leaders that you have been following, going to jail for, crying crocodile tears for. And they're nothing but Frank James and Jesse James and the what-do-you-call-'em bothers.

As soon as they got the setup organized, the white man made available to them top public-relations experts; opened the news media across the country at their disposal, which then began to project these Big Six as the leaders of the march. Originally they weren't even in the march. You were talking this march talk on Hastings Street, you were talking march talk on Lenox Avenue, and on Fillmore Street, and on Central Avenue, and 32nd Street and 63rd Street. That's where the march talk was being talked. But the white man put the Big Six at the head of it; made them the march. They became the march. They took it over. And the first move they made after they took it over, they invited Walter Reuther, a white man; they invited a priest, a rabbi, and an old white preacher, yes, an old white preacher. The same white element that put Kennedy into power — labor, the Catholics, the Jews, and liberal Protestants; the same clique that put Kennedy in power, joined the march on Washington.

It's just like when you've got some coffee that's too black, which means it's too strong. What do you do? You integrate it with cream, you make it weak. But if you pour too much cream in it, you won't even know you ever had coffee. It used to be hot, it becomes cool. It used to be strong, it becomes weak. It used to wake you up, now it puts you to sleep. This is what they did with the march on Washington. They joined it. They didn't integrate it, they infiltrated it. They joined it, became a part of it, took it over. And as they took it over, it lost its militancy. It ceased to be angry, it ceased to be hot, it ceased to be uncompromising. Why, it even ceased to be a march. It became a picnic, a circus. Nothing but a circus, with clowns and all. You had one right here in Detroit — I saw it on television — with clowns leading it, white clowns and black clowns. I know you don't like what I'm saying, but I'm going to tell you anyway. Because I can prove what I'm saying. If you think I'm telling you wrong, you bring me Martin Luther King and A. Philip Randolph and James Farmer and those other three, and see if they'll deny it over a microphone.

No, It was a sellout. It was a takeover. When James Baldwin came in from Paris, they wouldn't let him talk, because they couldn't make him go by the script. Burt Lancaster read the speech that Baldwin was supposed to make; they wouldn't let Baldwin get up there, because they know Baldwin is liable to say anything. They controlled it so tight, they told those Negroes what time to hit town, how to come, where to stop, what signs to carry, what song to sing, what speech they could make, and what speech they couldn't make; and then told them to get out of town by sundown. And every one of those Toms was out of town by sundown. Now I know you don't like my saying this. But I can back it up. It was a circus, a performance that beat anything Hollywood could ever do, the performance of the year. Reuther and those other three devils should get an Academy Award for the best actors because they acted like they really loved Negroes and fooled a whole lot of Negroes. And the six Negro leaders should get an award too, for the best supporting cast.

(Breitman 1990: 4-17)

● 「OAAUの基本方針と目的」

先に述べたように、マルコムXは「イスラムの民」脱退後「ムスリム・モスク」(宗教的な新団体) を設立、そしてメッカ巡礼に始まる中東、アフリカ諸国歴訪後、「OAAU (アフリカ系アメリカ人統一機構)」という名の非宗教的な新しい運動組織を作り上げます。

次の演説 (「The Founding Rally of OAAU」) は、1964年6月28日、ニューヨークのオーデュボン・ボールルームで開かれた「OAAU」最初の公開集会で行われたものです。彼はこのとき2つの演説をし、これはその1つ目にあたります。その内容は、彼自身ではなく新組織の委員会によって起草された草案「アフリカ系アメリカ人統一機構の基本方針と目的」を読み上げると同時に彼自身の解説を加えたものです。この中で取り上げられた主題は、マルコムXの死後「全国の黒人共同社会の中で基本的要求、プログラムとして提起され、闘われたテーマ」でもあります。このときの聴衆はやはり黒人大衆が中心であったようです。

Salaam Alaikum, Mr. Moderator, our distinguished guests, brothers and sisters, our friends and our enemies, everybody who's here.

As many of you know, last March when it was announced that I was no longer in the Black Muslim movement, it was pointed out that it was my intention to work among the 22 million non-Muslim Afro-Americans and to try and form some type of organization, or create a situation where the young people — our young people, the students and others — could study the problems of our people for a period of time and then come up with a new analysis and give us some new ideas and some new suggestions as to how to approach a problem that too many other people have been playing around with for too long. And that we would have some kind of meeting and determine at a later date whether to form a black nationalist party or a black nationalist army.

There have been many of our people across the country from all walks of life who have taken it upon themselves to try and pool their ideas and to come up with some kind of solution to the problem that confronts all of our people. And tonight we are here to try and get an understanding of what it is they've come up with.

Also, recently when I was blessed to make a religious pilgrimage to the holy city of Mecca where I met many people from all over the world, plus spent many weeks in Africa trying to broaden my own scope and get more of an open mind to look at the problem as it actually is, one of the things that I realized, and I realized this even before going over there, was that our African brothers have gained their independence faster than you and I here in America have. They've also gained recognition and respect as human beings much faster than you and I.

Just ten years ago on the African continent, our people were colonized. They were suffering all forms of colonization, oppression, exploitation, degradation, humiliation, discrimination, and every other kind of -ation. And in a short time, they have gained more independence, more recognition, more respect as human beings than you and I have. And you and I live in a country which is supposed to be the citadel of education, freedom, justice, democracy, and all of those other pretty-sounding words.

So it was our intention to try and find out what it was our African brothers were doing to get results, so that you and I could study what they had done and perhaps gain from that study or benefit from their experiences. And my traveling over there was designed to help to find out how.

One of the first things that the independent African nations did was to form an organization called the Organization of African Unity. This organization consists of all independent African states who have reached the agreement to submerge all differences and combine their efforts toward eliminating from the continent of Africa colonialism and all vestiges of oppression and exploitation being suffered by African people. Those who formed the organization of African states have differences. They represent probably every segment, every type of thinking. You have some leaders that are considered Uncle Toms, some leaders who are considered very militant. But even the militant African leaders were able to sit down at the same table with African leaders whom they considered to be Toms, or Tshombes, or that type of character. They forgot their differences for the sole purpose of bringing benefits to the whole. And whenever you find people who can't forget their differences, then they're more interested in their personal aims and objectives than they are in the conditions of the whole.

Well, the African leaders showed their maturity by doing what the American white man said couldn't be done. Because if you recall when it was mentioned that these African states were going to meet in Addis Ababa, all of the Western press began to spread the propaganda that they didn't have enough in common to come together and to sit down together. Why, they had Nkrumah there, one of the most militant of the African leaders, and they had Adoula from the Congo. They had Nyerere there, they had Ben Bella there, they had Nasser there, they had Sékou Touré, they had Obote; they had Kenyatta — I guess Kenyatta was there, I can't remember whether Kenya was independent at that time, but I think he was there. Everyone was there and despite their differences, they were able to sit down and form what was known as the Organization of African Unity, which has formed a coalition and is working in conjunction with each other to fight a common enemy.

Once we saw what they were able to do, we determined to try and do the same thing here in America among Afro-Americans who have been divided by our enemies. So we have formed an organization known as the Organization of Afro-American Unity which has the same aim and objective — to fight whoever gets in our way, to bring about the complete independence of people of African descent here in the Western Hemisphere, and first here in the United States, and bring about the freedom of these people by any means necessary.

That's our motto. We want freedom by any means necessary. We want justice by any means necessary. We want equality by any means necessary. We don't feel that in 1964, living in a country that is supposedly based upon freedom, and supposedly the leader of the free world, we don't think that we should have to sit around and wait for some segregationist congressmen and senators and a President from Texas in Washington, D. C., to make up their minds that our people are due now some degree of civil rights. No, we want it now or we don' t think anybody should have it.

The purpose of our organization is to start right here in Harlem, which has the largest concentration of people of African descent that exists anywhere on this earth. There are more Africans in Harlem than exist in any city on the African continent. Because that's what you and I are — Africans. You catch any white man off guard in here right now, you catch him off guard and ask him what he is, he doesn't say he's an American. He either tells you he's Irish, or he's Italian, or he's German, if you catch him off guard and he doesn't know what you're up to. And even though he was born here, he'll tell you he's Italian. Well, if he's Italian, you and I are African — even though we were born here.

So we start in New York City first. We start in Harlem and by Harlem we mean Bedford-Stuyvesant, any place in this area where you and I live, that's Harlem — with the intention of spreading throughout the state, and from the state throughout the country, and from the country throughout the Western Hemisphere. Because when we say Afro-American, we include everyone in the Western Hemisphere of African descent. South America is America. Central America is America. South America has many people in it of African descent. And everyone in South America of African descent is an Afro-American. Everyone in the Caribbean, whether it's the West Indies or Cuba or Mexico, if they have African blood, they are Afro-Americans. If they're in Canada and they have African blood, they're Afro-Americans. If they're in Alaska, though they might call themselves Eskimos, if they have African blood, they're Afro-Americans.

So the purpose of the Organization of Afro-American Unity is to unite everyone in the Western Hemisphere of African descent into one united force. And then, once we are united among ourselves in the Western Hemisphere, we will unite with our brothers on the motherland, on the continent of Africa. So to get right with it, I would like to read you the "Basic Aims and Objectives of the Organization of Afro-American Unity," started here in New York, June, 1964.

"The Organization of Afro-American Unity, organized and structured by a cross section of the Afro-American people living in the United States of America, has been patterned after the letter and spirit of the Organization of African Unity which was established at Addis Ababa, Ethiopia, in May of 1963.

"We, the members of the Organization of Afro-American Unity, gathered together in Harlem, New York:

"Convinced that it is the inalienable right of all our people to control our own destiny;

"Conscious of the fact that freedom, equality, justice and dignity are central objectives for the achievement of the legitimate aspirations of the people of African descent here in the Western Hemisphere, we will endeavor to build a bridge of understanding and create the basis for Afro-American unity;

"Conscious of our responsibility to harness the natural and human resources of our people for their total advancement in all spheres of human endeavor;

"Inspired by our common determination to promote understanding among our people and cooperation in all matters pertaining to their survival and advancement, we will support the aspirations of our people for brotherhood and solidarity in a larger unity transcending all organizational differences;

"Convinced that, in order to translate this determination into a dynamic force in the cause of human progress conditions of peace and security must be established and maintained;" — And by "conditions of peace and security," [we mean] we have to eliminate the barking of the police dogs, we have to eliminate the police clubs, we have to eliminate the water hoses, we have to eliminate all of these things that have become so characteristic of the American so-called dream. These have to be eliminated. Then we will be living in a condition of peace and security. We can never have peace and security as long as one black man in this country is being bitten by a police dog. No one in the country has peace and security.

"Dedicated to the unification of all people of African descent in this hemisphere and to the utilization of that unity to bring into being the organizational structure that will project the black people's contributions to the world;

"Persuaded that the Charter of the United Nations, the Universal Declaration of Human Rights, the Constitution of the United States and the Bill of Rights are the principles in which we believe and that these documents if put into practice represent the essence of man-kind's hopes and good intentions;

Desirous that all Afro-American people and organizations should henceforth unite so that the welfare and well-being of our people will be assured;

"We are resolved to reinforce the common bond of purpose between our people by submerging all of our differences and establishing a nonsectarian, constructive program for human rights;

"We hereby present this charter.

"I — Establishment.

"The Organization of Afro-American Unity shall include all people of African descent in the Western Hemisphere, as well as our brothers and sisters on the African continent." Which means anyone of African descent, with African blood, can become a member of the Organization of Afro-American Unity, and also any one of our brothers and sisters from the African continent. Because not only it is an organization of Afro-American unity meaning that we are trying to unite our people in the West, but it's an organization of Afro-American unity in the sense that we want to unite all of our people who are in North America, South America, and Central America with our people on the African continent. We must unite together in order to go forward together. Africa will not go forward any faster than we will and we will not go forward any faster than Africa will. We have one destiny and we've had one past.

In essence, what it is saying is instead of you and me running around here seeking allies in our struggle for freedom in the Irish neighborhood or the Jewish neighborhood or the Italian neighborhood, we need to seek some allies among people who look something like we do. It's time now for you and me to stop running away from the wolf right into the arms of the fox, looking for some kind of help. That's a drag.

"II — Self Defense.

"Since self-preservation is the first law of nature, we assert the Afro-American's right to self-defense.

"The Constitution of the United States of America clearly affirms the right of every American citizen to bear arms. And as Americans, we will not give up a single right guaranteed under the Constitution. The history of unpunished violence against our people clearly indicates that we must be prepared to defend ourselves or we will continue to be a defenseless people at the mercy of a ruthless and violent racist mob.

"We assert that in those areas where the government is either unable or unwilling to protect the lives and property of our people, that our people are within our rights to protect themselves by whatever means necessary." I repeat, because to me this is the most important thing you need to know. I already know it. "We assert that in those areas where the government is either unable or unwilling to protect the lives and property of our people, that our people are within our rights to protect themselves by whatever means necessary."

This is the thing you need to spread the word about among our people wherever you go. Never let them be brainwashed into thinking that whenever they take steps to see that they're in a position to defend themselves that they're being unlawful. The only time you' re being unlawful is when you break the law. It's lawful to have something to defend yourself. Why, I heard President Johnson either today or yesterday, I guess it was today, talking about how quick this country would go to war to defend itself. Why, what kind of a fool do you look like, living in a country that will go to war at the drop of a hat to defend itself, and here you've got to stand up in the face of vicious police dogs and blue-eyed crackers waiting for somebody to tell you what to do to defend yourself!

Those days are over, they're gone, that's yesterday. The time for you and me to allow ourselves to be brutalized nonviolently is *passé*. Be nonviolent only with those who are nonviolent to you. And when you can bring me a nonviolent racist, bring me a nonviolent segregationist, then I'll get nonviolent. But don't teach me to be nonviolent until you teach some of those crackers to be nonviolent. You've never seen a nonviolent cracker. It's hard for a racist to be nonviolent. It's hard for anyone intelligent to be nonviolent. Everything in the universe does something when you start playing with his life, except the American Negro. He lays down and says, "Beat me, daddy."

So it says here: "A man with a rifle or a club can only be stopped by a person who defends himself with a rifle or a club." That's equality. If you have a dog, I must have a dog. If you have a rifle, I must have a rifle. If you have a club, I must have a club. This is equality. If the United States government doesn't want you and me to get rifles, then take the rifles away from those racists. If they don't want you and me to use clubs, take the clubs away from the racists. If they don't want you and me to get violent, then stop the racists from being violent. Don't teach us nonviolence while those crackers are violent. Those days are over.

"Tactics based solely on morality can only succeed when you are dealing with people who are moral or a system that is moral. A man or system which oppresses a man because of his color is not moral. It is the duty of every Afro-American person and every Afro-American community throughout this country to protect its people against mass murderers, against bombers, against lynchers, against floggers, against brutalizers and against exploiters."

I might say right here that instead of the various black groups declaring war on each other, showing how militant they can be cracking each other's heads, let them go down South and crack some of those crackers' heads. Any group of people in this country that has a record of having been attacked by racists — and there's no record where they have ever given the signal to take the heads of some of those racists — why, they are insane giving the signal to take the heads of some of their ex-brothers. Or brother X's, I don't know how you put that.

"Ⅲ — Education

"Education is an important element in the struggle for human rights. It is the means to help our children and our people rediscover their identity and thereby increase their self-respect. Education is our passport to the future, for tomorrow belongs only to the people who prepare for it today."

And I must point out right there, when I was in Africa I met no African who wasn't standing with open arms to embrace any Afro-American who returned to the African continent. But one of the things that all of them have said is that every one of our people in this country should take advantage of every type of educational opportunity available before you even think about talking about the future. If you're surrounded by schools, go to that school.

"Our children are being criminally shortchanged in the public school system of America. The Afro-American schools are the poorest-run schools in the city of New York. Principals and teachers fail to understand the nature of the problems with which they work and as a result they cannot do the job of teaching our children." They don't understand us, nor do they understand our problems; they don't. "The textbooks tell our children nothing about the great contributions of Afro-Americans to the growth and development of this country."

And they don't. When we send our children to school in this country they learn nothing about us other than that we used to be cotton pickers. Every little child going to school thinks his grandfather was a cotton picker. Why, your grandfather was Nat Turner; your grandfather was Toussaint L'Ouverture; your grandfather was Hannibal. Your grandfather was some of the greatest black people who walked on this earth. It was your grandfather's hands who forged civilization and it was your grandmother's hands who rocked the cradle of civilization. But the textbooks tell our children nothing about the great contributions of Afro-Americans to the growth and development of this country.

"The Board of Education's integration plan is expensive and unworkable; and the organization of principals and supervisors in New York City's school system has refused to support the Board's plan to integrate the schools, thus dooming it to failure before it even starts.

"The Board of Education of this city has said that even with its plan there are 10 percent of the schools in Harlem and the Bedford-Stuyvesant community in Brooklyn that they cannot improve." So what are we to do? "This means that the Organization of Afro-American Unity must make the Afro-American community a more potent force for educational self-improvement.

"A first step in the program to end the existing system of racist education is to demand that the 10 percent of the schools the Board of Education will not include in its plan be turned over to and run by the Afro-American community itself." Since they say that they can't improve these schools, why should you and I who live in the community, let these fools continue to run and produce this low standard of education? No, let them turn those schools over to us. Since they say they can't handle them, nor can they correct them, let us take a whack at it.

What do we want? "We want Afro-American principals to head these schools. We want Afro-American teachers in these schools." Meaning we want black principals and black teachers with some textbooks about black people. "We want textbooks written by Afro-Americans that are acceptable to our people before they can be used in these schools.

"The Organization of Afro-American Unity will select and recommend people to serve on local school boards where school policy is made and passed on to the Board of Education." And this is very important.

"Through these steps we will make the 10 percent of the schools that we take over educational showplaces that will attract the attention of people from all over the nation." Instead of them being schools turning out pupils whose academic diet is not complete, we can turn them into examples of what we can do ourselves once given an opportunity.

"If these proposals are not met, we will ask Afro-American parents to keep their children out of the present inferior schools they attend. And when these schools in our neighborhood are controlled by Afro-Americans, we will then return our children to them.

"The Organization of Afro-American Unity recognizes the tremendous importance of the complete involvement of Afro-American parents in every phase of school life. The Afro-American parent must be willing and able to go into the schools and see that the job of educating our children is done properly." This whole thing about putting all of the blame on the teacher is out the window. The parent at home has just as much responsibility to see that what's going on in that school is up to par as the teacher in their schools. So it is our intention not only to devise an education program for the children, but one also for the parents to make them aware of their responsibility where education is concerned in regard to their children.

"We call on all Afro-Americans around the nation to be aware that the conditions that exist in the New York City public school system are as deplorable in their cities as they are here. We must unite our efforts and spread our program of self-improvement through education to every Afro-American community in America.

"We must establish all over the country schools of our own to train our own children to become scientists, to become mathematicians. We must realize the need for adult education and for job retraining programs that will emphasize a changing society in which automation plays the key role. We intend to use the tools of education to help raise our people to an unprecedented level of excellence and self-respect through their own efforts.

"IV — Politics and Economics."

And the two are almost inseparable, because the politician is depending on some money; yes, that's what he's depending on.

"Basically, there are two kinds of power that count in America: economic power and political power, with social power being derived from those two. In order for the Afro-Americans to control their destiny, they must be able to control and affect the decisions which control their destiny: economic, political, and social. This can only be done through organization.

"The Organization of Afro-American Unity will organize the Afro-American community block by block to make the community aware of its power and its potential; we will start immediately a voter registration drive to make every unregistered voter in the Afro-American community an independent voter."

We won't organize any black man to be a Democrat or a Republican because both of them have sold us out. Both of them have sold us out; both parties have sold us out. Both parties are racist, and the Democratic Party is more racist than the Republican Party. I can prove it. All you've got to do is name everybody who's running the government in Washington, D. C., right now. He's a Democrat and he's from either Georgia, Alabama, Texas, Mississippi, Florida, South Carolina, North Carolina, from one of those cracker states. And they've got more power than any white man in the North has. In fact, the President is from a cracker state. What's he talking about? Texas is a cracker state, in fact, they'll hang you quicker in Texas than they will in Mississippi. Don't you ever think that just because a cracker becomes president he ceases being a cracker. He was a cracker before he became president and he's a cracker while he's president. I'm going to tell it like it is. I hope you can take it like it is.

"We propose to support and organize political clubs, to run independent candidates for office, and to support any Afro-American already in office who answers to and is responsible to the Afro-American community." We don't support any black man who is controlled by the white power structure. We will start not only a voter registration drive, but a voter education drive to let our people have an understanding of the science of politics so they will be able to see what part the politician plays in the scheme of things; so they will be able to understand when the politician is doing his job and when he is not doing his job. And any time the politician is not doing his job, we remove him whether he's white, black, green, blue, yellow or whatever other color they might invent.

"The economic exploitation in the Afro-American community is the most vicious form practiced on any people in America." In fact, it is the most vicious practiced on any people on this earth. No one is exploited economically as thoroughly as you and I, because in most countries where people are exploited they know it. You and I are in this country being exploited and sometimes we don't know it. "Twice as much rent is paid for rat-infested, roach-crawling, rotting tenements."

This is true. It costs us more to live in Harlem than it costs them to live on Park Avenue. Do you know that the rent is higher on Park Avenue in Harlem than it is on Park Avenue downtown? And in Harlem you have everything else in that apartment with you — roaches, rats, cats, dogs, and some other outsiders — disguised as landlords. "The Afro-American pays more for food, pays more for clothing, pays more for insurance than anybody else." And we do. It costs you and me more for insurance than it does the white man in the Bronx or somewhere else. It costs you and me more for food than it does them. It costs you and me more to live in America than it does anybody else, and yet we make the greatest contribution.

You tell me what kind of country this is. Why should we do the dirtiest jobs for the lowest pay? Why should we do the hardest work for the lowest pay? Why should we pay the most money for the worst kind of food and the most money for the worst kind of place to live in? I'm telling you we do it because we live in one of the rottenest countries that has ever existed on this earth. It's the system that is rotten; we have a rotten system. It's a system of exploitation, a political and economic system of exploitation, of outright humiliation, degradation, discrimination — all of the negative things that you can run into, you have run into under this system that disguises itself as a democracy, disguises itself as a democracy. And the things that they practice against you and me are worse than some of the things that they practiced in Germany against the Jews. Worse than some of the things that the Jews ran into. And you run around here getting ready to get drafted and go someplace and defend it. Someone needs to crack you up 'side your head.

"The Organization of Afro-American Unity will wage an unrelenting struggle against these evils in our community. There shall be organizers to work with our people to solve these problems, and start a housing self-improvement program." Instead of waiting for the white man to come and straighten out our neighborhood, we'll straighten it out ourselves. This is where you make your mistake. An outsider can't clean up your house as well as you can. An outsider can't take care of your children as well as you can. An outsider can't look after your needs as well as you can. And an outsider can't understand your problems as well as you can. Yet you're looking for an outsider to do it. *We* will do it or it will never get done.

"We propose to support rent strikes." Yes, not little, small rent strikes in one block. We'll make Harlem a rent strike. We'll get every black man in this city; the Organization of Afro-American Unity won't stop until there's not a black man in the city not on strike. Nobody will pay any rent. The whole city will come to a halt. And they can't put all of us in jail because they've already got the jails full of us.

Concerning our social needs — I hope I'm not frightening anyone. I should stop right here and tell you if you're the type of person who frights, who gets scared, you should never come around us. Because we'll scare you to death. And you don't have far to go because you're half dead already. Economically you're dead — dead broke. Just got paid yesterday and dead broke right now.

"V — Social.

"This organization is responsible only to the Afro-American people and the Afro-American community." This organization is not responsible to anybody but us. We don't have to ask the man downtown can we demonstrate. We don't have to ask the man downtown what tactics we can use to demonstrate our resentment against his criminal abuse. We don't have to ask his consent; we don't have to ask his endorsement; we don't have to ask his permission. Anytime we know that an unjust condition exists and it is illegal and unjust, we will strike at it by any means necessary. And strike also at whatever and whoever gets in the way.

"This organization is responsible only to the Afro-American people and community and will function only with their support, both financially and numerically. We believe that our communities must be the sources of their own strength politically, economically, intellectually, and culturally in the struggle for human rights and human dignity.

"The community must reinforce its moral responsibility to rid itself of the effects of years of exploitation, neglect, and apathy, and wage an unrelenting struggle against police brutality." Yes. There are some good policemen and some bad policemen. Usually we get the bad ones. With all the police in Harlem, there is too much crime, too much drug addiction, too much alcoholism, too much prostitution, too much gambling.

So it makes us suspicious about the motives of Commissioner Murphy when he sends all these policemen up here. We begin to think that they are just his errand boys, whose job it is to pick up the graft and take it back downtown to Murphy. Anytime there's a police commissioner who finds it necessary to increase the strength numerically of the policemen in Harlem and, at the same time, we don't see any sign of a decrease in crime, why, I think we're justified in suspecting his motives. He can't be sending them up here to fight crime, because crime is on the increase. The more cops we have, the more crime we have. We begin to think that they bring some of the crime with them.

So our purpose is to organize the community so that we ourselves — since the police can't eliminate the drug traffic, we have to eliminate it. Since the police can't eliminate organized gambling, we have to eliminate it. Since the police can't eliminate organized prostitution and all of these evils that are destroying the moral fiber of our community, it is up to you and me to eliminate these evils ourselves. But in many instances, when you unite in this country or in this city to fight organized crime, you'll find yourselves fighting the police department itself because they are involved in the organized crime. Wherever you have organized crime, that type of crime cannot exist other than with the consent of the police, the knowledge of the police and the cooperation of the police.

You'll agree that you can't run a number in your neighborhood without the police knowing it. A prostitute can't turn a trick on the block without the police knowing it. A man can't push drugs anywhere along the avenue without the police knowing it. And they pay the police off so that they will not get arrested. I know what I'm talking about — I used to be out there. And I know you can't hustle out there without police setting you up. You have to pay them off.

The police are all right. I say there's some good ones and some bad ones. But they usually send the bad ones to Harlem. Since these bad police have come to Harlem and have not decreased the high rate of crime, I tell you brothers and sisters it is time for you and me to organize and eliminate these evils ourselves, or we'll be out of the world backwards before we even know where the world was.

Drug addiction turns your little sister into a prostitute before she gets into her teens; makes a criminal out of your little brother before he gets in his teens — drug addiction and alcoholism. And if you and I aren't men enough to get at the root of these things, then we don't even have the right to walk around here complaining about it in any form whatsoever. The police will not eliminate it. "Our community must reinforce its moral responsibility to rid itself of the effects of years of exploitation, neglect, and apathy, and wage an unrelenting struggle against police brutality."

Where this police brutality also comes in — the new law that they just passed, the no-knock law, the stop-and-frisk law, that's an anti-Negro law. That's a law that was passed and signed by Rockefeller. Rockefeller with his old smile, always he has a greasy smile on his face and he's shaking hands with Negroes, like he's the Negro's pappy or granddaddy or great-uncle. Yet when it comes to passing a law that is worse than any law that they had in Nazi Germany, why, Rockefeller couldn't wait till he got his signature on it. And the only thing this law is designed to do is make legal what they've been doing all the time.

They've passed a law that gives them the right to knock down your door without even knocking on it. Knock it down and come on in and bust your head and frame you up under the disguise that they suspect you of something. Why, brothers, they didn't have laws that bad in Nazi Germany. And it was passed for you and me, it's an anti-Negro law, because you've got an anti-Negro governor sitting up there in Albany — I started to say Albany, Georgia — in Albany, New York. Not too much difference. Not too much difference between Albany, New York, and Albany, Georgia. And there's not too much difference between the government that's in Albany, New York, and the government in Albany, Georgia.

"The Afro-American community must accept the responsibility for regaining our people who have lost their place in society. We must declare an all-out war on organized crime in our community; a vice that is controlled by policemen who accept bribes and graft must be exposed. We must establish a clinic, whereby one can get aid and cure for drug addiction."

This is absolutely necessary. When a person is a drug addict, he's not the criminal; he's a victim of the criminal. The criminal is the man downtown who brings this drug into the country. Negroes can't bring drugs into this country. You don't have any boats. You don't have any airplanes. You don't have any diplomatic immunity. It is not you who is responsible for bringing in drugs. You're just a little tool that is used by the man downtown. The man that controls the drug traffic sits in city hall or he sits in the state house. Big shots who are respected, who function in high circles — those are the ones who control these things. And you and I will never strike at the root of it until we strike at the man downtown.

"We must create meaningful, creative, useful activities for those who were led astray down the avenues of vice.

"The people of the Afro-American community must be prepared to help each other in all ways possible; we must establish a place where unwed mothers can get help and advice." This is a problem, this is one of the worst problems in our . . .

[*A short passage is lost here as the tape is turned.*]

"We must set up a guardian system that will help our youth who get into trouble." Too many of our children get into trouble accidentally. And once they get into trouble, because they have no one to look out for them they're put in some of these homes where others who are experienced at getting in trouble are. And immediately it's a bad influence on them and they never have a chance to straighten out their lives. Too many of our children have their entire lives destroyed in this manner. It is up to you and me right now to form the type of organizations wherein we can look out for the needs of all of these young people who get into trouble, especially those who get into trouble for the first time, so that we can do something to steer them back on the right path before they go too far astray.

"And we must provide constructive activities for our own children. We must set a good example for our children and must teach them to always be ready to accept the responsibilities that are necessary for building good communities and nations. We must teach them that their greatest responsibilities are to themselves, to their families and to their communities.

"The Organization of Afro-American Unity believes that the Afro-American community must endeavor to do the major part of all charity work from within the community. Charity, however, does not mean that to which we are legally entitled in the form of government benefits. The Afro-American veteran must be made aware of all the benefits due to him and the procedure for obtaining them."

Many of our people have sacrificed their lives on the battlefront for this country. There are many government benefits that our people don't even know about. Many of them are qualified to receive aid in all forms, but they don't even know it. But *we* know this, so it is our duty, those of us who know it, to set up a system wherein our people who are not informed of what is coming to them, we inform them, we let them know how they can lay claim to everything that they've got coming to them from this government. And I mean you've got much coming to you. "The veterans must be encouraged to go into business together, using GI loans," and all other items that we have access to or have available to us.

"Afro-Americans must unite and work together. We must take pride in the Afro-American community, for it is our home and it is our power," the base of our power.

"What we do here in regaining our self-respect, our manhood, our dignity and freedom helps all people everywhere who are also fighting against oppression."

Lastly, concerning culture and the cultural aspect of the Organization of Afro-American Unity.

" 'A race of people is like an individual man; until it uses its own talent, takes pride in its own history, expresses its own culture, affirms its own selfhood, it can never fulfill itself.' "

"Our history and our culture were completely destroyed when we were forcibly brought to America in chains. And now it is important for us to know that our history did not begin with slavery. We came from Africa, a great continent, wherein live a proud and varied people, a land which is the new world and was the cradle of civilization. Our culture and our history are as old as man himself and yet we know almost nothing about it."

This is no accident. It is no accident that such a high state of culture existed in Africa and you and I know nothing about it. Why, the man knew that as long as you and I thought we were somebody, he could never treat us like we were nobody. So he had to invent a system that would strip us of everything about us that we could use to prove we were somebody. And once he had stripped us of all human characteristics — stripped us of our language, stripped us of our history, stripped us of all cultural knowledge, and brought us down to the level of an animal — he then began to treat us like an animal, selling us from one plantation to another, selling us from one owner to another, breeding us like you breed cattle.

Why, brothers and sisters, when you wake up and find out what this man here has done to you and me, you won't even wait for somebody to give the word. I'm not saying all of them are bad. There might be some good ones. But we don't have time to look for them. Not nowadays.

"We must recapture our heritage and our identity if we are ever to liberate ourselves from the bonds of white supremacy. We must launch a cultural revolution to unbrainwash an entire people." A cultural revolution. Why, brothers, that's a crazy revolution. When you tell this black man in America who he is, where he came from, what he had when he was there, he'll look around and ask himself, "Well, what happened to it, who took it away from us and how did they do it?" Why, brothers, you'll have some action just like that. When you let the black man in America know where he once was and what he once had, why, he only needs to look at himself now to realize something criminal was done to him to bring him down to the low condition that he's in today.

Once he realizes what was done, how it was done, where it was done, when it was done, and who did it, that knowledge in itself will usher in your action program. And it will be by any means necessary. A man doesn't know how to act until he realizes what he's acting against. And you don't realize what you're acting against until you realize what they did to you. Too many of you don't know what they did to you, and this is what makes you so quick to want to forget and forgive. No, brothers, when you see what has happened to you, you will never forget and you'll never forgive. And, as I say, all of them might not be guilty. But most of them are. Most of them are.

"Our cultural revolution must be the means of bringing us closer to our

African brothers and sisters. It must begin in the community and be based on community participation. Afro-Americans will be free to create only when they can depend on the Afro-American community for support, and Afro-American artists must realize that they depend on the Afro-American community for inspiration."

Our artist — we have artists who are geniuses; they don't have to act the Stepin Fetchit role. But as long as they're looking for white support instead of black support, they've got to act like the old white supporter wants them to. When you and I begin to support the black artists, then the black artists can play that black role. As long as the black artist has to sing and dance to please the white man, he'll be a clown, he'll be clowning, just another clown. But when he can sing and dance to please black men, he sings a different song and he dances a different step. When we get together, we've got a step all our own. We have a step that nobody can do but us, because we have a reason for doing it that nobody can understand but us.

"We must work toward the establishment of a cultural center in Harlem, which will include people of all ages and will conduct workshops in all of the arts, such as film, creative writing, painting, theater, music, and the entire spectrum of Afro-American history.

"This cultural revolution will be the journey to our rediscovery of ourselves. History is a people's memory, and without a memory man is demoted to the level of the lower animals." When you have no knowledge of your history, you're just another animal; in fact, you're a Negro; something that's nothing. The only black man on earth who is called a Negro is one who has no knowledge of his history. The only black man on earth who is called a Negro is one who doesn't know where he came from. That's the one in America. They don't call Africans Negroes.

Why, I had a white man tell me the other day, "He's not a Negro." Here the man was black as night, and the white man told me, "He's not a Negro, he's an African." I said, "Well, listen to him." I knew he wasn't, but I wanted to pull old whitey out, you know. But it shows you that they know this. You are Negro because you don't know who you are, you don't know what you are, you don't know where you are, and you don't know how you got here. But as soon as you wake up and find out the positive answer to all these things, you cease being a Negro. You become somebody.

"Armed with the knowledge of our past, we can with confidence charter a course for our future. Culture is an indispensable weapon in the freedom struggle. We must take hold of it and forge the future with the past."

And to quote a passage from *Then We Heard the Thunder* by John Killens, it says: " 'He was a dedicated patriot: Dignity was his country, Manhood was his government, and Freedom was his land.' " Old John Killens.

This is our aim. It's rough, we have to smooth it up some. But we're not trying to put something together that's smooth. We don't care how rough it is. We don't care how tough it is. We don't care how backward it may sound. In essence it only means we want one thing. We declare our right on this earth to be a man, to be a human being, to be respected as a human being, to be given the rights of a human being in this society, on this earth, in this day, which we intend to bring into existence by any means necessary.

(Breitman 1992: 35-56)

第3章　あるがままの国際理解

●「国際理解教育」の実践者

　語学、特に公教育における外（国）語教育の目的の一部として、異文化理解とか国際理解がしばしば挙げられてきたことはご存じだと思います。外（国）語教育だけでなく、最近では社会科や小学校の総合の時間などでも「国際理解教育」の名の下にいくつもの取り組みがなされています。

　ただ「国際理解教育」(「国際理解」を促進する教育？) と言っても、では具体的にどのような教育なのかという点に関してはそのとらえ方は様々です。異文化理解、平和教育、国際教育、人権教育、開発教育、環境教育、これらすべてが国際理解教育ということばに包括される、あるいは少なくとも部分的に重なり合うと考えてもよいでしょう。そのことを踏まえながら、たとえば和田勝明氏は「国際理解教育」を次のように定義づけています。(1999：2)

「自国や自分が属する文化だけでなく他国や異文化を理解する中で、平和と人類の福祉のために諸問題を解決・改善しようとするための教育」

　さてここで、前章のマルコムXのことばや彼がしようとしたことを思い出してみて下さい。彼を一人の教育者として見るとき、彼はまさに「国際理解教育」の実践者であったと言えないでしょうか。彼がしていたことは、「自国（米国）や自分が属する文化（アフリカ系米国人文化）だけでなく、他国（アフリカ諸国）や異文化（米国白人文化やアフリカ諸民族文化）を理解する中で、平和と人類の福祉のために諸問題（人権問題、貧困問題）を解決・改善しようとするための教育（演説、運動）」ではなかったでしょうか。

　「いや、彼は教育者ではなく扇動家だ」とか「仮にそういうこじつけができ

るとしても、彼は暴力に訴えようとした。教育の方法を誤っている」と思われる方もおられるかもしれません。しかし、どのような「教育」であっても別の価値観を持った人から見れば「扇動」となり得ますし、「教育」の方法は1つであるはずがありません。ある教育（扇動？）の目的を達成する過程で、多種多様な方法論があることはむしろ自然で、どの方法でなければならないなんてことはないのです。またどの方法が効果的であったかということも、あとになって初めて言えることであって、実際それが行われているときには往々にして分からないものです。彼は、そのときその場では自衛（暴力ではない）を訴えることが米国黒人にも白人にも最も効果があると信じていただけなのです。非暴力を訴え続けたキング牧師もマルコムXと同様に殺されてしまったことを思い出せば、方法論の「優劣」は一概に決められないことが分かります。

いずれにせよ、マルコムXを国際理解教育実践の1つのモデルとして見ることは可能だと思われます。ですから読者の方々は前章を通じて、英語で（日本語の解説も交えながら）国際理解教育の典型例を読んできたことになります。地理や歴史で得られるような一知識としてだけでなく、つまり米国史のごく一面としてだけでなく、国際理解教育の実践者としてマルコムXを見るとき、私たち自身が国際理解（教育）を試みる際に指針となる姿勢（態度）、方法、ものの見方がそこに示されていることに気づくでしょう。

そこで本章では、もう一度マルコムXの活動を振り返りながら、彼の足跡のどのような点が私たち自身の国際理解（教育）に応用できるのかを考えてみたいと思います。

● あるがままの「人権国家」

マルコムXの活動を「国際理解教育」の実践とみなしてまず見えてくるのは、当然のことながら米国の「あるがままの姿」です。「人権」を国家的な基本概念の1つとし、あたかも人権擁護の先導者のようにも見られている米国においてアフリカ系米国人がどのような扱いを受けてきたかが、彼の生の声を通して浮き彫りにされています。

読者の方の中には、マルコムXやキング牧師らの活動そして死によって米国がすっかり変わり、今では理想的な人権国家になっているかのような印象を持つ人もいるかもしれません。しかし、あたりまえのことながら、過去は現在につながっています。確かに、キング牧師らを中心とする公民権運動の後、アフリカ系米国人は法的に対等の権利が認められ、実質的にも政治をはじめとする様々な分野で活躍する人の数が格段に増えました。ところがその一方で貧困層もむしろ増加していることは先に引用したとおり（第2章参照）であり、人種間の軋轢が解消されたとは言い難い状況が今でも続いているのが、米国のあるがままの姿なのです。それを裏付けるものとして、新聞に報道されるだけでも、人種差別にかかわる事件が次々と起こっています。一例を示しましょう。

黒人女性射殺の白人警官ら不起訴　米で人種対立激化　「偏見に基づく発砲」の声も
1999.05.12　産経新聞東京朝刊　4頁　国際2面　写有　（全1324字）
　【ロサンゼルス10日＝鳥海美朗】ニューヨークで白人警官による無実の黒人移民青年の射殺事件をきっかけに大規模な騒動が3月に起きたのに続き、今度は西海岸ロサンゼルス東郊のリバーサイド市で黒人女性を誤って射殺した白人警官らが不起訴になったことで、米国内の人種対立が激化している。10日には同市内で600人以上がデモ行進する抗議運動が展開され、40人以上が逮捕された。背景には黒人ら人種的少数派を「潜在的犯罪者」とみる警察側の体質がからんでおり、尾を引きそうだ。
　リバーサイド市で10日繰り広げられた集会やデモ行進には、黒人を中心とする地域の市民グループや宗教関係者らが参加した。デモ行進は市役所前から郡検事局、警察へと続き、「殺人をどう正当化しようというのか」といったプラカードが並んだ。
　3月にニューヨーク市警前で展開された、大規模な抗議運動に参加した黒人指導者シャープトン師も今回のデモに参加。連邦政府に対し、事件にかかわった警官4人の起訴を要求する演説を行った。デモの世話人らは「非暴力」行動を呼びかけたが、警官ととなり合ったり、びんを投げたりする参加者もおり、シャープトン師を含む40数人が公務執行妨害容疑などで逮捕された。
　事件が起きたのは昨年12月28日未明。リバーサイド市内のガソリンスタンドの駐車場内で、ドアをロックされた車の中に黒人女性のタイーシャ・ミラーさん（当時19歳）が意識混濁状態になっているのをいとこの通報でかけつけた警官4人が発見した。
　検事局の調べによると、ミラーさんのひざの上には銃があり、警官4人が車の

窓ガラスを破ったところ、「ミラーさんが銃に手をのばしたため、自己防衛だ」として発砲したという。計23発のうち頭などに12発を浴びたミラーさんは即死した。

この事件では、発砲した警官4人はいずれも白人。目撃者が警官が「クロ（黒人）を早く車から出せ」「イヌをけしかけろ」などと叫ぶのを聞いており、「人種差別の偏見にもとづく発砲」との強い批判が起きた。2月には、黒人指導者ジャクソン師も参加する大規模なデモが行われた。だが、リバーサイド郡検事局は6日、警官の発砲を「状況判断の誤り」としたものの「（殺人容疑での）有罪を立証する十分な証拠がない」として4人の不起訴処分を発表。ミラーさんの遺族や黒人市民らが抗議の意思を表明していた。

リバーサイド郡は人口（約120万人）の7割を白人が占め、黒人は1割足らず。ミラーさんのいとこで10日の抗議デモを組織した1人、バーネル・バトラー師は産経新聞に、「不起訴は、みえすいた事件のもみ消しだ。1999年の今、なおもこんな事件が起きたことが悲しい。（連邦政府の）リノ司法長官に、事件についての公正な調査の実施を求める」と語った。

ニューヨークでは今年2月、犯罪とは無関係のギニア（アフリカ）系移民の青年が白人警官4人から40発以上の銃弾を浴びて死亡する事件があった。「職権乱用」と問題になり、ニューヨーク市警には連日黒人市民らのデモが押しかけ、1,200人以上が逮捕される騒動になった。

　人種間対立の潜在的担い手となるのは一部の「横暴な」白人警官だけではありません。公然と白人至上主義を唱え、黒人に対するリンチを平気で過去行っていた「ＫＫＫ」は、規模は縮小してはいても現在も存在しますし、かつてマルコムＸがその一員として活躍した「イスラムの民」も、マルコムＸに勧誘されて入団したルイス・ファラカーン師を指導者として、一部で反発を受けながらもアフリカ系米国人の間で大きな影響力を持ちつつあります。たとえば西暦1995年にはワシントンで黒人男性だけによる「100万人大行進」を主催し、キング牧師らの「ワシントン大行進」の規模（約25万人）を上回る約80万人（40万人ともいわれる）の黒人男性を集めました。また翌年ファラカーン師はリビア訪問時にリビアの最高指導者カダフィ大佐が制定した「カダフィ人権賞」を受け取っています。さらに、「イスラムの民」主催の「100万人大行進」の影響を受け、1997年にペンシルベニア州フィラデルフィアでは、黒人女性の「100万人大行進」と銘打った大規模な集会が行われ、女性数十万人が参加しています。

今日も米国では人種間の偏見や対立が至る所に見られ、根本的な問題は何も解決されていない状況にあるようにも思えます。余談になりますが、マルコムX個人にまつわる事件も未だに起こっています。次の記事は、毎日新聞（1997年8月10日、国際面）に載せられたものです。

・［揺れる夏］97アメリカ／6　悲劇のマルコムX一家　夫人の死招いた「暗殺」の影
　　12歳の少年は四角い箱で顔を隠され警察の車から降りた。10人以上のカメラマンが撮影する。ニューヨーク州ヨンカースの家庭裁判所に入っていった。
　　容疑は殺人。6月1日、ヨンカースの祖母の家に放火し、祖母は全身やけどで同23日死亡した。全米の関心を集めたのは、亡くなったベティ・シャバズさん（63）が戦闘的な黒人運動指導者マルコムXの夫人だったからだ。
　　1965年2月、夫が暗殺された。シャバズさんは、6人の女の子を育てながら大学院に通い、75年には教育経営学の博士号をとった。大学の管理部門に勤め、各地で講演して夫の理想を語り継いだ。苦境にあっても努力して地位をつかみ、家族を守る。夫とは別の意味で黒人社会を代表する女性だった。
　　そんなシャバズさんに、孫の少年がなぜ火をつけたのか。少年の弁護を担当する前ニューヨーク市長、デービッド・ディンキンズさんに尋ねると、「問題を抱えた子なんだ。母親が暗殺を目撃した」と短く答えた。
　　少年の母はマルコムXの二女、クビラさん（36）。4歳の時、父親が射殺され血だらけになっているのを見た。心の傷が彼女の人生を不安定にした。95年、黒人イスラム教徒組織、ネーション・オブ・イスラムの指導者、ルイス・ファラカン師殺害を計画した疑いで起訴された。
　　同師が暗殺に関与したのではとの疑惑が当時からあり、クビラさんは父の敵討ちを考えたのだった。検察は専門家のカウンセリングを受けることを条件に起訴を取り下げた。
　　クビラさんは少年をシャバズさんに預け、自分はテキサス州で人生をやり直そうと試みた。今年初め、少年が同居するようになったが、母子の関係はつまずく。2月、クビラさんは「息子が暴れている」と警察を呼んだ。少年は、母が酒を飲んで酔っ払ったと答えた。
　　5月、少年は再び祖母の家に戻された。そして、ガソリンをまき火をつけた。
　　スパイク・リー監督の映画「マルコムX」（92年）を契機にマルコムXが再評価されている。背景には「いかなる手段を取ろうとも」とマルコムXがアフリカ系米国人の権利を主張して30年以上たった今でも、差別の残る現実がある。
　　マルコムXの暗殺はクビラさんの心に消えない傷を残し、母の病んだ心は少年に不安定な心と行動をもたらし、シャバズさんの死につながった。悲劇が悲劇を呼ぶ。少年には8日、最低1年半の少年院収容の決定が下された。マルコム家の

ドラマは終わらない。

　考えてみればマルコムXは西暦1925年の生まれですから、もし生きていれば2001年現在で76歳なのです。歴史上の人物どころか私たちと時代を共有する人であり、彼の生きた時代は過去ではなく現在だと言ってもよいでしょう。

　さらに付け加えておきましょう。視点を米国から世界へ移すと、差別問題どころか奴隷制を未だに残している地域すら存在しています。次の記事を見て下さい。

Selling Sudan's Slaves Into Freedom
By IAN FISHER
April 25, 1999, Sunday *The New York Times*

Over the last few years, evidence has slowly solidified that slavery not only exists, but may be widespread in parts of Sudan. On a recent day in this tiny, scorching village, there seemed little to dispute that. Seated under trees, were several hundred women and children. They told stories of abduction and rape and tending goats for their captors.

But there has been growing scrutiny over the kind of transaction that followed.

"That's 1 million," John Eibner, a quietly intense American, said as he reached into a bag fat with Sudanese money. "That's 2 million."

He was counting out cash to pay a trader for 535 of the slaves, Dinka people from the south taken captive by Arabs from the north. The cost: 26.8 million Sudanese pounds, about $27,000, or $50 a person, the price of two goats. In a week, Eibner, an official with a Swiss group called Christian Solidarity International, bought freedom for 1,783 slaves — by far the greatest number since he started coming to Sudan in 1995.

As the number of redeemed slaves and groups trekking to the war zone of southern Sudan to free them has risen, the practice is coming under fire. Critics say that redemption, which began locally in the early 1990s, is becoming big business, and that people like Eibner may even be inadvertently encouraging slave raids.

"Once the numbers started to increase drastically, that caused people who follow the slavery issue to have a look at what is really going on," said Jemera Rone, counsel for Human Rights Watch in Washington.

Ms. Rone recently wrote a paper accusing the Sudanese government of using slave raids as a weapon in its 15-year war with southern rebels and warning of the danger of redemption. She worries that unscrupulous middlemen — traders who bring the slaves back south — may increase profits by packing groups of slaves with "borrowed" children, and that peace in Sudan may be discouraged if raiders have a financial incentive to keep the war going.

Last month, the U.N. Children's Fund also raised some questions, partly in response to the American school children, in Massachusetts, Colorado and Oregon, who raise money for the cause.

"We want to try to deal with ending slavery as a fundamental change within Sudan, rather than having to watch human beings being bought and sold," said Stephen Lewis, UNICEF's deputy executive director.

He said UNICEF officials were working with Sudan — which denies slavery exists but concedes "tribal" hostage-taking — to allow a study of slavery and mechanism for freeing captives. "We have to get rid of the practice, period," he said. "We need a political solution."

Caroline Cox, who runs a British group that redeems slaves, acknowledged that redemptions were "a gray area" but said they were unavoidable. "We justify it by saying: It's not the answer but I don't think you can look a child in the face and say, 'I'm sorry, you have to remain a slave until there is a political solution,'" she said.

Eibner, whose group claims to have freed 7,725 slaves since 1995, also sees redemptions as imperfect but necessary.

"Knowing that tens of thousands of people are still enslaved and knowing that we can get them out," he said, "I couldn't live with myself and say, 'Sorry, I'm stopping because of some criticism from an ivory tower in London or New York.'" Eibner, 46, is a native of Valhalla, N.Y., who lives in Geneva.

50ドルを米ドルとすると、1人の人間が5,000円余りで売り買いされていることになります。この報道が「事実」なら、現在でも世界には奴隷制が存在していると言えます。

こうしてみると、公民権闘争、人権運動、あるいは奴隷制ですら、過去の出来事ではなく、私たちが生きている現在の問題であるし、「人権擁護の先進国」とされる米国も含め世界中のどこでも、時間的、質的違いはあれ、人権その他の諸問題は解決などしていない現状がまず認識できると思います。もちろん日本も例外ではありません。このことは国際理解教育を明らめる出発点となります。

● 国家を越えて

　「国を越え、民族を越え、文化を越えて、お互いが偏見なく理解し合いましょう」という漠然とした呼びかけは確かに「国際理解」と見なせるのですが、上で挙げた「国際理解教育」の定義はもう少し踏み込んだ解釈が必要になると思われます。それは具体的な方法ないしは方向性を含むものです。すなわち、他国や他文化圏で起こっている問題を見据え、自国や自文化圏の問題を見直し、一国家や一文化圏で解決できない問題を認識することに加え、その具体的な解決策や方法を模索するところまで含んでいるという解釈です。

　この意味でマルコムXが晩年に採った運動の手法は、国際理解教育が採り得る具体的な方法を明確に示していることになり、注目に値します。前章で見たとおり、彼は、「公民権」を「人権」の問題にまで高めることを主張しました。「公民権」は国家内の問題にすぎず、米国という一国家内ではアフリカ系米国人はいつまでたっても少数派であり劣勢を免れない。それを「人権」問題ととらえることによってはじめて国家を越えた組織との連携が可能になると。具体的にはOAUや国連などの国際的な組織を指しますが、それらの組織からの外圧で米国政府を変えることを彼は試みたのです。一国家内では少数派であっても、国家の枠組みを越える「普遍的な」概念を前面に出し、国際的な協力を得ることにより多数派ないしは拮抗した勢力に転じる。この手法は、国際理解教育を進める際の基本的方向性の1つを示していると言えましょう。

● あるがままの国際理解教育

　ただし、ここで同時に確認すべきは、この手法には限界があり必ずしも成功するとは限らないということです。現に、マルコムがOAUに提出した案は結果として国連の会議で発表されずに終わっています。このことは国際理解教育の前提に関して、2つの点で重要な示唆を与えてくれるように思えます。1つは、「国際的組織」の「力」を過信することの危うさであり、もう1つは人類普遍の

概念があると盲信することの不適切さです。

　「一国で解決できない問題は国連などの国際的機関に持ち込む」という発想は国際理解教育において妥当かつ自然ではありますが、その限界も同時に認識しておく必要があります。国際的機関の代表格である国連をまず考えてみましょう。

　マルコムXが「世界」の代名詞として国連を意識していたように、日本においても国連というものは非常に重視され、国家の政策にも教育にも大きな影響を及ぼします。多くの日本人の意識では、もしかするとマルコムX以上に、国連を「世界政府的かつ中立的」、「国家よりも優先するべきもの」ととらえる傾向が強いようにも見受けられます。

　確かに国連は、世界中のほとんどの国が加盟し（西暦2000年9月5日現在で加盟国数189か国）、一国単位では解決できない多くの問題を処理できる数少ない組織の1つではあります。しかし、しばしば指摘されるとおり、国連は「世界政府」でもなければ、完全に「中立」でもありません。

　そもそも「国際連合」という訳語自体が、特にその「中立性」に関して誤解を生む原因の1つになっているのかもしれません。英語では「United Nations」ですが、その語が本来どのような意味を持つか、次の定義の2番目を見て下さい。

United Nations n. [the ～]
1 [〈sg.〉] 国際連合 《1945年組織; 略 UN; cf. → LEAGUE OF NATIONS》.
2 [〈pl.〉]《第2次大戦の枢軸国 (the Axis) に対する》連合国《26国》.
(『リーダーズ英和辞典』(1997))

　「連合国」は、日本にとって第2次世界大戦で戦った相手、つまり敵国の集まりです。戦後、戦勝国である「連合国（United Nations）」が中心となって「国際連合（United Nations）」を作ったのです。日本語で別々の訳語をあてているため、あたかもまったく別の組織であるかのように誤解しがちですが、英語では「連合国」と「国際連合」は、まったく同じものを指すわけではないに

せよ、両者は直結しています。現に今でも『国連憲章』には「敵国条項」と呼ばれる条項が残っており、当然日本もその「敵国」に含まれています。次の条項を見れば、国名こそ明記していませんが、日本、ドイツ、イタリアの枢軸国および第2次大戦中枢軸国側に属したハンガリー、ルーマニア、ブルガリア、フィンランドを指すことは明らかです。

Article 53

The Security Council shall, where appropriate, utilize such regional arrangements or agencies for enforcement action under its authority. But no enforcement action shall be taken under regional arrangements or by regional agencies without the authorization of the Security Council, with the exception of measures against any enemy state, as defined in paragraph 2 of this Article, provided for pursuant to Article 107 or in regional arrangements directed against renewal of aggressive policy on the part of any such state, until such time as the Organization may, on request of the Governments concerned, be charged with the responsibility for preventing further aggression by such a state.

The term enemy state as used in paragraph 1 of this Article applies to any state which during the Second World War has been an enemy of any signatory of the present Charter.

Article 107

Nothing in the present Charter shall invalidate or preclude action, in relation to any state which during the Second World War has been an enemy of any signatory to the present Charter, taken or authorized as a result of that war by the Governments having responsibility for such action.

それら（旧）敵国は現在ではすべて国連に加盟し「世界平和」に貢献しているにもかかわらず、また再三その事実を踏まえて条項の削除を主張しているにもかかわらず、この敵国条項は戦後50年以上経過した今でも削除されていませ

ん。

　国連が「中立」でないことは、この「敵国」条項が存在することだけでも分かりますし、他にも永世「中立」国のスイスが加盟していないことからも分かります。スイスは、国連に対して特定の活動に限って参加する場合もありますが、現在でも加盟国ではないのです。

　また国連が「国家よりも優先すべきもの」、「世界政府」でもないことは、最近の米国や英国の動きを見てもよく分かります。西暦1991年、イラクに対する軍事力行使が米軍を中心とする多国籍軍によって行われました。このときの軍事介入は国連決議によるものであり、米国、英国も国連を重要視しているように見えます。これに対して、1999年に行われた米国、英国を中心とするNATO（北大西洋条約機構）軍のユーゴ爆撃はどうでしょうか。このときロシアや中国は「国際法違反」と「主権国家侵害」の観点から非難しましたし、欧米諸国内でも反対論者は、NATOが国連安保理（安全保障理事会）の承認を経ず、しかも集団自衛の範囲を超えた軍事介入を主権国家に対して行ったことを批判しました。空爆当時国連安保理はユーゴ非難決議は出していましたが、軍事行動の承認はしてなかったようです。国連が「許して」もいないのにNATO軍は「人道上」の理由で爆撃したのです。つまりこれは、加盟国が、ある時には国連で決議されたことを理由に軍事行動を起こし、別のあるときには国連決議より他のことを優先させて行動を起こす典型的な例と見ることができましょう。

　さらに、『国連憲章』には米国の主張で入ったとされる次のような規定があります。第43条の3項です。

> The agreement or agreements shall be negotiated as soon as possible on the initiative of the Security Council. They shall be concluded between the Security Council and Members or between the Security Council and groups of Members and shall be subject to ratification by the signatory states in accordance with their respective constitutional processes.

　安全保障理事会で決定が下ると、非軍事的強制措置は例外なしに、軍事的な強制措置も基本的に加盟国はそれに従うことになりますが、軍事的措置の場合、

上の条項により、各国がそれぞれ憲法上の手続きに従って批准することになります。これは、ユーゴ空爆のときとは逆にもし国連安保理で決議された軍事行動であっても、加盟国は必ずしも加わらなくともよいことを意味します。(浅井 1993: 27)

　要するに国連は、加盟国が都合のよいときだけ利用し、場合によっては無視、あるいは脱退することさえ可能な、組合のようなものなのです。別のことばで言えば、「加盟国(主権国家)それぞれが利用できる道具」と理解することもできます。

　しかもこの道具は、全加盟国がまったく平等に利用できるものならまだよいのですが、一部の国だけに特権が与えられるような面も持っています。総会では確かに加盟国すべてがその政治形態や経済的状態にかかわらず同じ1票の投票権を持ち、「平等な」側面が見られます。しかし、国連の中核的存在として平和と安全保障の問題を扱う安全保障理事会においては、各国平等になっているとはとうてい言えません。15の理事国中、5か国(中国、フランス、ロシア連邦、英国、米国)だけが常任理事国であり、これらの国だけが特権を持ちます。「安全保障理事会で重要な決議を通過させるためには、9か国の理事国が賛成の投票をしなければなりませんが、5つの常任理事国のうち1か国でも反対票を投じた場合、これは拒否権と呼ばれて、決議は通過しないことになります。(http://www.unic.or.jp/know/orgf2.htm)」

　いわゆる国連そのものに加えて、国連の関連機関についても同様のことが言えます。そもそも「国際理解教育」ということばが広く使用されるようになったのは、西暦1954年第8回ユネスコ総会で採択された「国際理解と国際協力のための教育」からだそうですが、そのいわば世界大の「国際理解教育」のきっかけを作ったユネスコ(国連教育科学文化機関)という国際組織も状況は似ています。ユネスコは西暦1945年に設立された国連の専門機関であり、日本ユネスコ協会連盟(http://www.unesco.or.jp/gaiyo/yakume.htm)はその役目を次のようにまとめています。

　ユネスコのやくめは、お互いの無知や偏見をなくし(国際理解)、国や民族を越えて人びとが協力することを学び(国際協力)、人びとの友情と連帯心を育

てながら、共に生きる平和な地球社会を作っていくことです。

つまり、ユネスコという組織自体が、「国際理解」や「国際協力」を促すために存在するわけです。日本のユネスコ加盟は、国連加盟よりも5年も早い1951年であり、現在ではほぼ全都道府県で280ものユネスコ協会がユネスコ憲章に基づいた活動をしています。西暦1999年末には日本人の松浦晃一郎氏が第8代ユネスコ事務局長に任命されるなど、日本はユネスコに対して非常に積極的な貢献をしていると言えるでしょう。

あたかも教育関係の世界政府的役割を果たせそうなこのユネスコではありますが、母体である国連同様これもあくまで自主参加の協同組合のようなものです。ですから自国に不都合な決議などがある場合には脱退することも可能です。実際、英国や南アフリカなどはユネスコを脱退した時期がありましたし、米国は西暦1984年に脱退したままです。理由は当然ながらこの機関が自分たち主導で動かないことがあったからです。

国連をはじめとする国際組織のこのような「あるがままの姿」を明らめる必要があるように思われます。

次に普遍的概念の問題ですが、第1章で示したとおり、究極的には「これは普遍でこれは普遍でない」と分別すること自体が不可能です。普遍的と見なされる諸概念も、あくまである人間（集団）がある時代に置かれた環境の中で作り出したもの（フィクション）と言えるかもしれません。現在では、いわゆる「グローバル・スタンダード」と呼ばれる諸概念がそれに該当するでしょうか。「平和」、「自由」、「人権」などはあたかも世界中の人々が理想とし、求めるものであるかのように思えます。しかしながら、何が「平和」なのか、何が「自由」なのか、何が「人権」なのかという問いには一律の答えが返ってくるとはとても考えられません。個人の属する政治的、経済的、社会的、文化的、宗教的、そして言語的環境によって、その答えは様々であるはずです。

例として、マルコムXの運動の中心概念の1つであった「人権」について少し考えてみましょう。少なくとも米国における「人権」思想は、前章で見たように、人間を完全に超越した唯一絶対の神の存在が前提となります。つまり神を信じなければ、「人権は普遍だ」ということはできないのです。「人権」とと

もによく用いられる「平等主義」にしても同様に考えてよいかもしれません。『米国独立宣言』で見たように、すべての人々は平等に「創られた」ものであり、創造主（神）を前提としています。

しかるに、日本での「人権思想」それの基礎となる「平等思想」は、「神」を前提としていないように思えます。たとえば『日本国憲法』にある「人権」、「平等」は次のように規定されます。

第11条
　国民は、すべての基本的人権の享有を妨げられない。この憲法が国民に保障する基本的人権は、侵すことのできない永久の権利として、現在および将来の国民に与へられる。

第14条
　すべて国民は、法の下に平等であって、人種、信条、性別、社会的身分又は門地により、政治的、経済的又は社会的関係において、差別されない。

戦後ＧＨＱ草案の内容をほとんど変えることなく発布された憲法であるため米国人的な発想が随所に見られるにもかかわらず、「神」や「創造主」ということばは見あたりません。そのどころか、「憲法が国民に保障する基本的人権」、とか「法の下に平等」ということばが目立ち、「人間」が作った「国家」や「法律」が主体であるかのような解釈さえできます。もちろん、第11条の「侵すことのできない永久の権利」を見れば、その「普遍性」を顕しているのだと受け止めることは可能です。また実際日本人の多くが「人権」は普遍だと信じているようにも思えます。しかし、「なぜそれが普遍なのか」と聞かれたとき、多くの日本人は何と答えるでしょう。一神教を信じる人であれば、「神」をその根拠とするでしょうが、神と自然と人間の区別を明確に意識しない多くの人にとっては、「人権」の普遍性、絶対性の根拠を「神」以外に求めるか、「人権普遍説」そのものを否定するしか選択肢はないように思えます。

そうすると「人権思想」、そして「平等思想」はその根拠という点で、宗教や思想によってあるいは神を信じるかどうかによりその解釈が異なることは間違

いなさそうです。はっきり言えば、それらの思想は「普遍性」を持たないのです。「人権を普遍的なものということにしたい」とは言えても「人権は普遍的である」とは言えないのです。

　仮に、普遍的とまではいかなくとも「人権は大切」ということはすべての人が認めたとしましょう。その場合でさえも、何を人権とするか、何を人権問題とするかという認識が異なれば、理解や協力のしようがありません。普遍でない以上共通の認識は得られないと考える方が妥当であると言わざるを得ないでしょう。先に触れた「カダフィ人権賞」を権威ある賞だと認める人もいれば、鼻で笑う人もいるのではないでしょうか。

　「人権」だけでなくその他にも普遍的とされる概念は多々あります。もしかすると「民主主義」ということばも現代の日本では普遍的概念ととらえられるかもしれません。しかし、たとえば日本の「民主主義」と米国の「民主主義」とは同じ概念でしょうか。あるいは朝鮮民主主義人民共和国の「民主主義」とはどうでしょうか。もし異なるとすれば、どちらが「正しい」ものでどちらかが「正しくない」ものなのでしょうか。それをだれが決めることができるのでしょうか。

　このように、普遍的価値を持つと思われる概念でさえその認識が国により人により大きく異なるのが自然であるという意識を持っておくことは、国際理解教育の大きな前提の1つとなると考えられます。お互い完全に理解し合うことは、ほとんど不可能とさえ言えるのかもしれません。

● 国際理解（教育）を明らめる

　これまで述べてきたことを考えると、「国際理解（教育）」はそもそもできないこと、あるいは「夢」を追うようなことに思えるかもしれません。世界中至る所に存在する無数の「問題」、国際的組織の限界、普遍的概念の危うさ、そして国と国や人と人の間での「理解」や「協力」がほとんど不可能な場合もあるという現実を明らめることを薦めてきたのですから。しかし、だからと言って国際理解（教育）そのものを諦めようと言っているわけではありません。自分

も実践しようと望めば方法はいくつもあります。

　民族問題、宗教問題、環境問題、エネルギー問題、開発問題等々「国際社会」には解決すべきだと考えられる問題が山積みされています。そして実際にそれらの問題を解決すべく多くの活動がなされています。国連のような大きな組織だけでなく、様々な「市民レベル」での国際組織の取り組みも多々あります。国際組織の限界を知りながらその取り組みに積極的に貢献する。これも実践の1つでしょう。

　また、いわゆる「国際的な」取り組みにまで参加せずとも私たちの身の回りには、帰国子女問題、在日韓国・朝鮮の人たちをはじめとする登録外国人問題、留学生やその他の外国人との接触、原子力発電所の問題など、国際理解教育の課題となり得る問題がいくらでも存在します。これら日本国内の問題を認識し、それを解決する方法を模索する、そして具体的に行動すること、これもやはり国際理解教育の実践となります。

　ただし、もう既にお分かりでしょうが、特に国を越える活動の中にはいわば「価値や基準の押し付け」になってしまうものがしばしばあります。つまり国際問題解決のための活動がまた新たな国際問題を生む可能性があるということです。たとえば言語問題です。国際的な組織の運営はほとんどの場合単一または少数の「共通語」で行われます。その共通語が使えない者は活動に参加することすらできないし、参加できる言語運用力を持っていても中途半端な運用力では意見が反映されないということも起こります。意見を対等に反映させたいと思えば、その言語を習得するために一方的な負担を強いられることになります。第1章で述べた「言語権」の問題がここに生じるわけです。これは場合によってはそれこそ「人権問題」ともとらえられます。そのような観点から、国際的な活動自体に異議を唱えること、それに条件を付けること、あるいは敢えて参加を拒否することなども、「国際理解教育」の実践であると言えるかもしれません。

　いずれにせよ、物事をできる限り「明らめ」ることにより、自分がこだわりなく信じるものを得るのです。マルコムXは、自分自身を、黒人を、白人を、そして世界を明らめる試みを続けた結果「悪夢」を見ました。それにもかかわらず、いや、それだからこそ、心命に信ずるに至った「必要ないかなる手段を」

もとろうとすることにいささかのこだわりもなかったのです。この「明らめ」の態度こそが国際理解（教育）にも求められるのではないでしょうか。

　「必要ないかなる手段を」もとろうとすることは本質的に誰にも実現不可能なものです。本質的に実現不可能なものとは、平均的な人間にも実現（実践）できる道徳とは違い、まさに宗教的理想なのです。そして、そこにこそ実現不可能な理想が果たす現実的役割があるのです。すなわち、「必要ないかなる手段を」もとることを実践しようとすると、それは人間などには完全に遂行できない理想であることが自覚できるのです。そこにこそ、人間は人間の弱さが切実に自覚できるようになるのです。人間の弱さの自覚は、同時に、他人に対しては赦しとなって現れるものです。そこには正義・不正義の対立（こだわり）はなくなります。人間の弱きこと、人間に「絶対の正義」など持つことができないこと、すなわち人間のあるがままを自覚すること、これが現実的意義のある実現不可能な「あるがままの国際理解」なのです。

第4章　暗誦のすすめ

● こだわり（分別）のない「まるごと」

—— さまざまな文章を暗誦する ——
これが語学の王道、と言われます。
にもかかわらず、最近の語学ではとかく敬遠されているように思われます。
　もちろん、文章の暗誦だけが語学のすべてではありません。それに、暗誦という作業に慣れないうちはなかなか思うようにうまくいきません。ちょうど、自転車に初めて乗るときのように、慣れるまでは何度か転んだりするかもしれません。
　しかしながら、ある外（国）語を身につけるのに、その外語による文章の暗誦はとても役に立ちます。外語を習熟するために欠かすことのできない基礎訓練の1つと心得るべきものと言えるでしょう。
　また、文章の暗記をたくさん行うことによって「記憶」という行為に習熟することにもつながりますので、他の学習活動にも有効です。もちろん、記憶した文章はそのまま知識として学習者の資産となります。
　ここでいう「文章の暗誦」の肝心を一言で表現するならば
—— 言語を分別せず、まるごと身につける ——
ということです。
　「言語を分別せず」には、2つの意味を込めております。1つは、ある文章を読んだり聞いたりして「なかみ（意味）」を理解したとしても「かたち（音声や文字やその他）」も習得しなければ言語の習得ではない、ということです。
　文章の「なかみ」と「かたち」とは本来は不可分のものなのです。ですから文章の意味を理解したとしても、暗誦（音声や文字やその他）もできなければ文章の一側面しか学んでいないことになります。

「言語を分別せず」のもう1つの意味は、文法や語法などの言語に関する詳細な「知識」を通して文章を分析することから（意識的に）離れよ、ということです。

要するに
——一切は1つである——
という認識に立脚するのです。

言語と人間とは分離することはできませんし、人間と環境とは不可分でなのです。同じく、言語と環境も不可分です。そして、
——全体は部分の総和でない——
のです。ですから、単語を文法などで寄せ集めたのが本来の文章ではないのです。

ここでいう文章とは「文章まるごと」のことです。「文章まるごと」とは文章の「かたち（音声や文字やその他）」と「なかみ（意味）」の詳細にこだわりを持たない、ということです。そして言語と人間とそれを取りまく環境の「まるごと」が文章なのです。

たとえて言えば、ケーキをまるごと食べるときのことを想像して下さい。そのときその場（環境）であなたは、ただひたすらケーキを楽しめばよいのです。総カロリーがいくらだとか、ビタミンはどれくらいだとか、どこ産のイチゴがのっているだとか、生クリームに何パーセントの砂糖が入っている、マイセンの皿にのっている、銀製のフォークだ、この部屋はビクトリア調だ、などなどをいろいろ分析する必要はないのです。

ケーキ評論家ではなく、ただケーキを楽しむ人になればよいのです。ケーキは本来、食べて楽しむためにあるのですから。

語学も同じです。語学もほんらい、学ぼうとする言語によって表現されたケーキ（かたち〈音声や文字やその他〉、意味内容）を、そのときその場でまるごと楽しむべきものなのです。

そして、忘れてはいけないのは、ケーキを楽しむ「あなた」がいなければ、ケーキは楽しめないのです。

ここでいう暗誦を言い換えれば
——文章まるごと楽しむ——

ということになります。これは本書でいう暗誦の根本となる精神です。

　本章は英語の暗誦を読者にすすめるものです。英語暗誦の1つの方法を解説する手引書（マニュアル）と心得て下さい。

　繰り返し強調しますが、「さまざまな文章を暗誦する」ことは語学学習にたいへん役に立ちます。事実、読者が実際に試してみるとよく分かります。実行が実益を実証します。本書の暗誦例題のどれから始めてももかまいませんから、たとえ1つでもぜひ体験してみて下さい。（まずは、実行あるのみです）。

● 文章まるごと楽しむ

　「文章をまるごと暗誦！？　そんな無茶なぁ！！」このような叫び声を上げている人がいるかもしれませんが、そんなに心配はご無用です。

　何の手立てや工夫も凝らさずに「何とかして全部覚えて下さい！」などと勧めているわけではありません。何事も階段を上るがごとく一段上ってまた一段と確実に上るのが普通です。しかもこの階段はそんなに高くはないとすぐに感じるはずです。是非、ここで紹介する練習を試して下さい。

　前提になる学力は中学校などで習う基礎的な文法の力だけで十分です。読み方（発音）も最初から万全を心がけなくてもよいでしょう。思ったよりも苦労せずに多くの文章を短期間で確実に脳裏に焼き付け、何時でも口から出すことができるようになるはずです。あたかも幼い頃に口ずさんだ歌のように。（もちろん筆記やワープロ入力による演習でも構いません。）

　本章では暗誦例題として50話の「小話」（パンチ・ライン：punch line）を取り上げています。

　これらの「小話」はアメリカ国民一般の間で、人から人へと口頭で伝えられているもので、現代アメリカ文化における口承文芸といえるものです。どれもが最後の部分がオチ（ジョーク）になっています。

　ここで取り上げた「小話」はアメリカ国民の間で広く知られた模範的なものばかりですので、暗誦するほどまでに理解できたときには、同時にアメリカ英語を話す人々のものの見方や考え方（アメリカ人の「フィクション」）の一端を

垣間見ることができるでしょう。

　また、「小話」は人間の日常を題材とした話なので、「あまねく人間は、その弱さ（愚かさ）ゆえに慈悲と慈愛が必要である」ことが自然と素描されています。この意味においても

　── あまねく人間は平等 ──

であることを感じていただけると思います。

　さて、暗誦といっても単に機械的に「かたち（音声や文字）」のみが記憶できただけでは楽しくありません。聞かせどころ（読みどころ）と効果（パンチ）のある小話はあなたの頭脳への十分な刺激となるはずです。暗誦が自由自在にこなせるようになれたら、身につけた小話を自分自身で変幻自在に扱えるようにもなれる醍醐味を味わって下さい。

　本章では、あくまで暗誦の一方法を紹介するものです。ですから、「小話」に興味がない方は、方法だけを体得して下さい。

　そして、その方法が有効だと思われた方は、前章までに紹介した文章を含めどんどん自分の興味のある文書の暗誦に利用してみて下さい。また、方法も絶対のものではありません。読者おのおのが自身に適合するような方法にどんどん改良していただければよいのです。

● 「文の成り立ち」……自然に与えられた能力を活かそう

　「文の成り立ち」というと「文法」ということになるけれど、恐れることはありません。私たちはすでに自然に「文法」を習得済みなのです。ここから先の暗誦練習はすべて私たちがすでに与えられている能力を利用するものです。

　たとえば（1）のような動詞（＋助動詞および時制要素など）が与えられれば、すぐに文を作ることができるでしょう。

　（1）　a. 飛んでいる
　　　　b. 捕まえた
　　　　c. あげる（与える）だろう

平常文を基本と考え、どのようなものでもよいから平常文を作ると次の（2）のようになります。

(2) a. 赤トンボが飛んでいる。
　　b. ネコがネズミを捕まえた。
　　c. 飼育係はペンギンに小魚をあげるだろう。

　論より証拠、ここで直ちに実験です。(2) の部分だけ手で隠して下さい。そこに何が書いてありましたか？　思い出すのに少々時間がかかっている人も安心して、(1) を見て下さい。そうすると、直ぐに (2) に書いてあったことを思い出せたでしょう。
　これは文というものが命題と呼ばれる1つのまとまった意味内容で成り立っていることをすでに習得している証拠なのです。そして、命題の中核は動詞なのです。
　たとえば、「飛んでいる」という部分だけが会話のなかで聞き取れたらすぐに「何（誰）が？」と思うし、「捕まえた」ならば「何（誰）が？　何（誰）を？」と思うし、「あげるだろう」ならば「誰（何）が？　誰（何）に？　何を？」とすぐ思うのです。「飛んでいる」が聞き取れて「誰（何）が？　誰（何）に？　何を？」と思う人はいないでしょう。
　すなわち、動詞が決定されれば、その「文の成り立ち」を私たちの心が自動的に見積もり（compute）してくれるのです。
　この能力はことばを用いる人間に共通に備わっているのです。日本語と英語とでは、文の内部構造が違っていても、ある命題の意味内容を表すという機能は同じです。ですから、ここで暗誦しようとしている英語の文章にも利用できるのです。
　試しに次の (3) の英文を意味が理解できるまで読んでください。

(3) a. The woman was running.
　　b. Mr. Yamada has spent all of his salary.

c. My boss will put her luggage in the car.

　さて、ここで（3）を見ないで、（4）を見て下さい。（4）は（3）のそれぞれの文から動詞（＋助動詞および時制要素など）のみを抜き出したものですが、これを参照すると容易に（3）の英文を思い出す（心の中で再構成する）ことができるはずです。（この方法に少し慣れるまで時間がかかるかもしれません。練習あるのみ！）

　（4）　a. was running
　　　　b. has spent
　　　　c. will put

　いかがでしたか？　（4）は（3）の情報量のおよそ1/4程度だと思われますが、残りの3/4は自動的ともいうべき容易さで脳裏によみがえり、（4）の文のとおりに再構成できたと思います。少し時間が経ってから（4）を見ても同じように再構成できるはずです。
　ここから先、このように文中の部分情報のみを参照して全体を思い出す方法自体を「再構成」と呼ぶことにします。再構成は口頭と筆記（あるいはその他）とのどちらの場合をも意味します。
　長い文章になっても原理は同じです。文を積み重ねていけばよいだけです。
　文章中の動詞を中核として参照すれば、一度理解した文章はそれ以外のものは見なくとも容易に再構成することができるのです。これを繰り返し練習すれば知らず知らずのうちに（集中力はいりますが時間はそれほどかかりません）、まったく何も見なくてもその文章を暗誦することができるようになっているのです。

● 再構成とメモ

　ひととおり意味を理解した文章を再構成する原理は以上に説明したとおりです。でも実際には（3）のような単純ばかりではないですよね。たとえば（4）

の動詞部分は次の (5) のような文の主動詞部分にもなりますね。

(5) a. The woman whose husband I knew very well was running in the park.
b. Mr. Yamada, who is one of my coworkers, has spent all of his salary on his fishing boat.
c. My boss will not put her luggage in the car because she thinks it will easily become the target of robbery.

いくら何でもこれだけの情報量の文を最初から (4) の動詞部分だけで再構成するのはあまりにも酷です。
　ご安心下さい。実を言うと先ほどの原理だけで再構成できるようになるのは、暗誦を目指した練習の最終段階なのです。ですから実際はもっともっと簡単な段階、参照できる情報量の多い段階から始めて徐々に動詞部分のみの練習に近づけていくのです。
　ここからは、再構成のために参照する情報を「メモ」と呼ぶことにします。
　一番初めの段階では、基本的に動詞の他に「機能語」となっている語句をすべてメモに残してよいこととします。メモには概ね次の (6) に示したよう語句を記録できるものとします。

(6) ── メモの規準 ──

　　＜１＞動詞（＋助動詞や時制要素など）、
　　　　　be動詞の補語（もしくはbe動詞すぐ後の語(句)）、
　　　　　叙述形容詞、
　　　　　数字、
　　　　　yes / no、
　　　　　否定
　　＜２＞５Ｗ１Ｈ、
　　＜３＞接続詞、関係詞

＜4＞前置詞、to不定詞のto
　　＜5＞名詞句が大きい（長い）場合その主要名詞
　　　　　形容詞句が大きい（長い）場合その主要形容詞
　　＜6＞時や場所や理由、
　　　　　量、程度、頻度を示すもの
　　＜7＞その他必要に応じて

　これだけの情報量がメモにあれば、一応の理解をすませた文章を再構成することが容易にできます。そして徐々に＜7＞、＜6＞、＜5＞、＜4＞、＜3＞、＜2＞の情報を記録しないメモを用いて再構成する練習を繰り返し、＜1＞だけのメモで再構成できるように向上を図るのです。

　ちなみに、＜1＞には動詞部分に加えて、be動詞の場合にはその補語（これがないと何のことか分からない場合が多い）や補語以外のときはすぐ後の語（句）（先の理由と同じ：たとえば　The book is on the table. の場合であれば前置詞の　on）、叙述形容詞（これも先の理由と同じ）、そして数字（正確に記憶するのは困難）をメモに残してよいものとします。

　さらに絶対に必要な情報として肯定なのか否定なのかを示す yes や no　と否定辞の no、 not、 never　などもメモに残します。また、動詞は原型に戻さなくともよいものとし、それらを補う助動詞や時制や相（進行・完了）や態（能動・受動）などの意味を表す語句もそのまま「動詞部分」としてメモすることとします。

　それでは、ここまでの説明が直ちによく分からなかったとしても、以下の模範演習を行うことによって、メモを用いた再構成のやり方がすぐに理解できるようになりますので、さっそく練習を始めてみましょう。

● 「小話」の再構成、模範演習

　第1のステップです。まずは次の暗誦例題1.をよく読んで内容を理解して下さい。

本屋さんでの男性のお客さんと店員さんの会話です。お客さんがさがし求めている本のタイトルから想像できる本の実際の内容および分野と、その本に対する本屋さんの認識とに大きなズレが生じているところが理解の要です。
　アメリカ社会に生きる男性のはかなき夢、叶わぬ願望、最も頻繁にパンチ・ラインで取り上げられるネタの1つで、この暗誦例題1.はその典型ともいえるものです。ちなみに'fiction'とは「小説」の意味、つまり作り話、虚構や捏造という意味にもなる語です。

暗誦例題1.
A man goes into a bookstore and asks a clerk:
　"Do you have a book published recently
　'How to Control a Woman'?"
　"We certainly do," answers the clerk,
　"It's a best seller right now."
　"Can you tell me which shelf I will find it on?"
　"Well, of course it's on the fiction shelf."

　いかがですか？　最終行の店員さんのセリフが「おち」になっていたのが分かりましたでしょうか？　内容がよく理解できるまで読めれば第1の準備は完了です。
　次に第2のステップです。今度は上述の「メモの規準」に従ってメモを作成します。最初は＜1＞から＜4＞の規準までを全部含めたものを作成すればよいでしょう。＜5＞の規準も含めてもかまいませんが、よほどの困難さを感じない限りこれで十分のはずです。以後はこの＜1＞から＜4＞までの規準のメモを「標準メモ」と呼ぶことにします。
　　暗誦例題1.の標準メモのサンプルを次に示します。あくまでもサンプルですので、規準にさえ従っていれば様式は自由です。各自の好みに合わせてメモに残す語句の配列や整理をして下さい。

暗誦例題 1．　標準メモ例

_ ___ goes into _ _____ and asks _ _____:
　"Do ___ have _ ____ published _____
　'How to Control _ _____'?"
　"__ _____ do," answers ___ _____,
　"__'s a best seller _____ ___."
　"Can ___ tell __ which shelf _ will find __ on?"
　"____, of _____ __'s on ___ _____ _____."

　消えた単語の文字の代わりに ___ を付しておきました。文字1つに _ 1つが対応しています。カンマやピリオドなどの句読点はそのままに残してあります。It's のような It is の音声上の省略部分は、元に戻して is とはせずにそのまま 's と表示してあります。

　あくまでも暗誦を目指すための補助ですので、その他必要に応じて文の構造や構成を示す記号などを工夫して付け加えることは差し支えありません。もちろん、余計と思うものは削除すればよいのです。

　それでは、上記の標準メモだけを参照して暗誦例題1. が再構成できるようになるまで練習を重ねて下さい。

　標準メモで再構成できるようになったら、次のステップです。標準メモに記載した語句から、およそ＜4＞、＜3＞、＜2＞の規準の順番で少しずつ削除したメモを作成し、徐々に語句を削除したメモを参照しながら再構成ができるようになるまで練習を繰り返して下さい。そして、＜1＞の規準の語句だけを残したメモが最後の段階です。

　暗誦例題1.の再構成練習における最終ステップでのメモのサンプルを次に示しておきます。このようなメモを「最終メモ」と呼ぶことにします。

暗誦例題1.　最終メモ例

_ ___ goes into _ _____ ___ asks _ _____:
　"Do ___ have _ ____ published _____
　'___ __ Control _ _____?'"
　"__ _____ do," answers ___ _____,
　"__'s a best seller _____ ___."
　"Can ___ tell __ _____ _____ _ will find __ __?"
　"____, __ _____ __'s on ___ _____ _____."

　最終メモで十分に再構成できるようになったら、今度はメモなし、いよいよ暗誦への挑戦です。途中で失敗したらまた最終メモを見て再構成のやり直し。そしてまたメモなし。
　この作業を何度も繰り返せば、意外と簡単に完成度の高い安定した暗誦をすることができるようになるはずです。何度か暗誦ができてもさらに何回も繰り返し練習して下さい。「習うより慣れろ（Practice makes perfect.）」です。
　暗誦例題1.の暗誦はできるようになりましたでしょうか？　これで再構成の練習方法が理解できたと思います。それでは、以下の暗誦例題2.〜暗誦例題50.のパンチ・ラインもこの練習方法に基づいて1つずつ制覇していって下さい。（どこから始めてもかまいません）
　暗誦例題2.から暗誦例題10.まではそれぞれの標準メモをサンプルとして付記しておきました。

暗誦例題2.

After waiting a long time for his order, a customer calls for the waiter:
　"How long will my spaghetti be?"
The waiter answers:
　"Now that you mentioned it... I've never measured it before ... probably about eight inches."

162

暗誦例題 2.　標準メモ例
After waiting _ ____ ____ for ___ _____, _ _____ calls for ___ _____:
　"How long will __ _____ be?"
___ _____ answers:
　"Now that ___ mentioned __... _'ve never measured __ before ... _____ about eight _____."

暗誦例題 3.
A customer has been waiting for so long for his order that he finally calls over the waiter:
　"Hey, I ordered half a duck quite a while ago. Can you tell me when it's going to be ready?"
　"I'm sorry, sir. But you see... until someone else orders the other half of the duck, we can't very well kill one."

暗誦例題 3.　標準メモ例
_ _____ has been waiting for __ ____ for ___ _____ that __ _____ calls over ___ _____:
　"___, _ ordered half _ ____ _____ _ _____ ___.
　Can ___ tell __ when __'s going to be ready?"
　"_'m sorry, ___. But ___ see... until _____ ____ orders ___ _____ half of ___ ____, __ can't very well kill ___."

暗誦例題 4.
A passenger in a first-class cabin on a luxury cruise ship goes to complain to the attendant about the leak in the bathroom compartment. After carefully checking all the pipes and the faucets, the attendant finally decides the cause of the trouble.
　"Madam, it seems that the problem is not in the bath. It's the ship

that's leaking"

暗誦例題4. 標準メモ例

_ _____ in _ _____-_____ ____ on _ _____ _____ ____ goes to complain to ___ _____ about ___ ____ in ___ _____ _____. After _____ checking ___ ___ _____ and ___ _____, ___ _____ _____ decides ___ _____ of ___ _____.

"_____, __ seems that ___ _____ is not in ___ ____. __'s ___ ____ that's leaking"

暗誦例題5.

A lonely stranger takes a seat in a San Francisco restaurant:
　"May I take your order?" asks the waitress with a big smile.
　"Yes," answers the stranger. "I'd like two hamburgers and a kind word."
The waitress brings the man his hamburgers and is about to leave when he calls her back, saying:
　"Miss, I asked you for a word of kindness, too."
At that she smiles again and whispers in his ear:
　"If I were you, I wouldn't eat these hamburgers."

暗誦例題5. 標準メモ例

_ _____ _____ takes _ ____ in _ ___ _____ _____:
　"May _ take ____ _____?" asks ___ _____ with _ ___ _____.
　"Yes," answers ___ _____. "_'d like two _____.
　and _ ____ ____."
___ _____ brings ___ ___ ___ _____ and is about to leave when __ calls ___ back, saying:
　"Miss, _ asked ___ for _ ____ of _____, too."

At ____ ___ smiles _____ and whispers in ___ ___:
  "If _ were ___, _ wouldn't eat _____ _____."

暗誦例題 6.

A conversation at a cleaner's:

  "Hi, is the overcoat I brought in the other day ready?"
  "Yes, it is, sir."
  "That's seven dollars, right?"
  "I'm afraid I have to ask you for thirty dollars."
  "Hey, what's going on in here? The sign right up there says seven dollars for an overcoat, doesn't it?"
  "Yes, but I have to charge you for the five pairs of socks, the six handkerchiefs and the seven pairs of underpants that were stuffed into the pockets."

暗誦例題 6. 標準メモ例

_ _____ at _ _____'_:
  "__, is ___ _____ _ brought in ___ _____ ___ ready?"
  "Yes, __ is, ___."
  "____'s seven dollars, _____?"
  "_'m afraid _ have to ask ___ for thity _____."
  "___, what's going on in ____? ___ ____ _____ up _____ says seven _____ for __ _____, doesn't __?"
  "Yes, but _ have to charge ___ for ___ five _____ of _____, ___ six _____ and ___ seven _____ of _____ that were stuffed into ___ _____."

暗誦例題 7.

Late at night, a daughter calls home to her mother:

  "Mom, is it all right If I stay out a bit later tonight?"

"That depends on the reason, dear."
"Well, you see, about twenty of us are having a party,
  and if I leave, the party will die," explains the daughter.
"Well, if there're twenty people there, I don't see why
  your leaving will make such a difference."
"It will, mom, because I'm the only girl here."

暗誦例題 7. 標準メモ例
____ at _____, _ _____ calls home to ___ _____:
"___, is __ all right If _ stay out _ ___ _____ _____?"
"____ depends on ___ _____, ____."
"____, ___ see, about twenty of __ are having _ _____,
  and if _ leave, ___ _____ will die," explains ___ _____.
"____, if _____'re twenty _____ _____, _ don't see why
  ____ _____ will make ____ _ _____."
"__ will, ___, because _'m ___ only ____ ____."

暗誦例題 8.
At a railroad station a group of luggage handlers are worked loading a train's baggage car. But they throw the luggage in so roughly that a passing gentleman feels he should inform the station manager. The station manager thanks the man for going out of his way:
 "I'll go and give them a warning right away."
He hurries over to the baggage car and sees the gentleman has indeed been right:
 "Hey! Watch how you throw that stuff in!
   You're going to dent the baggage car!"

暗誦例題 8.　標準メモ例

At _ _____ _____ _ _____ of _____ _____ are worked loading _ _____'_ _____ ___. But ____ throw ___ _____ in so _____ that _ _____ _____ feels __ should inform ___ _____ _____. ___ _____ _____ thanks ___ ___ for going out of ___ ___:

　"_'ll go and give ____ _ _____ _____ ____."
__ hurries over to ___ _____ ___ and sees ___ _____ has _____ been right:

　"___ ! Watch how ___ throw ____ _____ in!
　___'re going to dent ___ _____ ___!"

暗誦例題 9.

Soon after marrying, Monica makes a disturbing discovery about her new husband Bill. She knew he was a baseball fan, but she has never thought his love of the game is so fanatical. Night and day all he thinks about is baseball, and he never pays any attention to her at all. One night, seeing her husband absorbed in another baseball broadcast on TV, Monica decides to have it out then and there:

　"Bill, I want to hear the truth. You love baseball more than
　　you love me, don't you?"
　"Well, maybe so, but you shouldn't get so upset.
　　I love you more than I love basketball or football."

暗誦例題 9.　標準メモ例

____ after marrying, _____ makes _ _____ _____ about ___ ___ _____ ____. ___ knew __ was a baseball fan, but ___ has never thought ___ ____ of ___ ____ is so fanatical. _____ and ___ all __ thinks about is _____, and __ never pays any _____ to ___ at all. ___ _____, seeing ___ _____ absorbed in _____ _____

第4章 暗誦のすすめ 167

_____ on __, _____ decides to have __ out ____ and _____:
 "____, _ want to hear ___ _____. ___ love _____ more than ___ love __, don't ___?"
 "____, maybe so, but ___ shouldn't get so upset.
 _ love ___ more than _ love _____ or _____."

暗誦例題10.

A newly wed man comes home from work one night. Greeting him at the door, his wife says:
 "Dear, I have wonderful news."
 "Oh, what is it?"
 "We're soon going to be a family of three."
 "Really? That is great news. Let's celebrate it with a toast."
While the husband goes to the liquor cabinet to prepare the toast, the wife calls home to her mother. "Mother, I told you there was no needs to worry. When I told George you were coming to live with us, he was delighted. In fact, he is fixing us a toast right now."

暗誦例題10. 標準メモ例

_ _____ ___ ___ comes home from ____ ___ _____. Greeting ___ at ___ ____, ___ ____ says:
 "____, _ have _____ ____."
 "__, what is __?"
 "__'re ____ going to be a family of three."
 "Really? ____ is great news. Let's celebrate __
  with _ _____."
While ___ _____ goes to ___ _____ _____ to prepare ___ _____, ___ ____ calls home to ___ _____.
 "_____, _ told ___ _____ was no needs to worry.
  When _ told _____ ___ were coming to live with __,

__ was delighted. In ____, __ is fixing __ _ _____ _____ ___."

以下の暗誦例題11.から暗誦例題50.まではメモを自分で作成してみましょう。
（6）の規準に従って、上の例にならってメモを作成して、再構成の練習をして下さい。あくまでも暗誦が最終目的なのであまり
——メモの様式にはこだわらない——
ようにして下さい。短い小話から少々長い小話まで、順番はどれからでもかまいませんから、「再構成」練習や「暗誦」練習を繰り返してして下さい。当然、筆記やワープロ入力など、暗誦の精神さえ生かしていれば、表現の形式は自由です。

暗誦例題11.
Bob was pleased with himself for finally getting a ticket to a popular Broadway play. When he got to the theater, it had a capacity crowd. But for some reason, the seat next to him was vacant even after the play started.
　"Gee, I wonder what happened to the person who bought this seat?" he said to the woman on the other side.
　"Well, it was my husband's, but he passed away recently," she answered.
　"Then you could have given it to one of your family or friends, couldn't you?"
　"No, you see, they're all at the funeral tonight."

暗誦例題12.
I was on a train once, and in the same compartment was a priest who seemed to be absorbed in a very difficult book. When the conductor came around to check our tickets, the priest began to search furiously through his pockets and case. The conductor said:
　"Reverend, there's no hurry. I'll check your ticket on the way

back."
But the priest continued to search frantically. I said:
"Didn't you hear what the conductor said? He said you could take your time to find it."
"Yes, that's all very well, but I'm afraid I won't know where I'm going till I see my ticket."

暗誦例題13.
A middle-aged couple checked in a Las Vegas hotel. The bellboy carried the luggage to the room, and before leaving, asked the gentleman:
"Is there anything else I can do for you?"
"That'll be all, thanks," said the man, handing him a tip.
Looking toward the woman as she disappeared into the bathroom:
"Is there anything I can get for your wife?"
Then, as if remembering something, the man said:
"Yes, I guess. I should at least send her a postcard. Will you buy me a postcard of Las Vegas."

暗誦例題14.
A conversation in a jewelry shop:
"Take a look at this," said the customer.
"Oh, yes, this is the ivory carving you purchased from us the other day," replied the shop owner.
"That's right. And at the very high price for that," snapped the customer.
"Not at all. I gave you a very reasonable price for this. Do you have any sort of complaint?"
"I sure do. I showed this to a friend who is an expert on ivory, and he said this is made of artificial ivory."

"You don't say."
"Well, it must be in India in these days that they're giving elephants false teeth too."

暗誦例題 15.

A stingy man held a taxi.
"How much will it cost to get to the station?"
"Well, from here, it'll cost twelve dollars."
The man said:
"I have some luggage here that I want to take?"
"Well, that looks a bit heavy. I'll charge you extra three dollars for that."
"O.K.. "
The man took some money out of the wallet.
"Here's three dollars. Just take the luggage. I'm going to walk myself. "

暗誦例題 16.

Mr. Armstrong always looked bent and was poorly dressed. His wife, however, had a beautiful figure and was always stylishly dressed. One day a friend of Mr. Armstrong was amazed when he saw his wife going shopping in a stunning outfit, all of latest fashions. Later he said to Mr. Armstrong:
"Your wife sure knows how to dress. She is really up on the times"
Mr. Armstrong answered dryly:
"As a matter of fact, she is three years ahead of the times"
"Three years? How do you know exactly?" asked his friend in disbelief.
"That woman has already spent all of my salary for the next

three years. That's how I know."

暗誦例題 17.

"I was told before coming this hotel had hot and cold running water. But my bathroom only has one faucet," complained the guest at the front desk.
"Of course it'll give you both hot and cold water. In the summer it gets very hot, and in the winter it gets as cold as ice."

暗誦例題 18.

Two businessmen were eating breakfast at a cafeteria. One said to the other after watching him bring back the other serving from the self-service counter.
　"You sure have a great appetite."
　"Yes, there's nothing I love more than eating. There're only
　two things I can't eat at breakfast."
　"Oh.. I wouldn't have thought there were things you couldn't
　eat. What are they?"
　"Lunch and dinner."

暗誦例題 19.

"Waiter, look here! My crab has only one pincher. What happened?"
"Let me explain, sir. You see our crabs here are so lively that they sometimes fight each other in our fresh tank."
"Well, in that case, take this one back and bring me the winner."

暗誦例題 20.

In front of a San Francisco department store, a TV camera had been set up, and the store president and staffs stood by it, apparently waiting for something. As a middle-aged gentleman approached the door, suddenly music began to blare and klieg lights shone on his face. A master of ceremony stepped forward and said to the bewildered man.

"Congratulations! You are the millionth customer to visit the store."

"Who? Me?"

"That's right. Now, will you tell us and our television audience what you came here for?"

"Yes, I'd be glad to. I just came to use the bathroom."

暗誦例題 21.

George was in constant fear of his wife, and he had a good reason to be. She was built like a pro wrestler and had a habit of showing off her strength. One day the couple went hiking. After reaching the camp site, his wife went for a walk while George dutifully began to prepare the dinner. A while later, a police officer came running up to George out of breath:

"We're chasing a bear that escaped from the zoo. But he got himself into the same cave as your wife went . . ."

Before the officer could even finish, George cut in:

"I'll tell you right now. If that bear suffers any injury, I'm not responsible."

暗誦例題 22.

A man was asking his wife what she wants for her birthday. She replies:

"I want a divorce."

The man replies:

"Gee, I wasn't planning on spending that much."

暗誦例題 23.

A farmer got sent to jail, and his wife was trying to keep the farm together until her husband was allowed to get out. She was not, however, very good at farm work, so she wrote a letter to him in jail:

"Dear sweetheart, I want to plant the pumpkins. When is the best time to do it?"

The farmer wrote back:

"Honey, don't go near that field. That's where all money and gold are buried."

But, because he was in jail all of the farmer's mail was censored. So when the sheriff and his deputies read this, they all ran out to the farm and dug up the entire pumpkin field looking for money and gold. After six full days of digging, they didn't find one single treasure. The farmer then wrote his wife:

"Honey, now is when you should plant the pumpkins."

暗誦例題 24.

An out-of-towner driving west on Geary Street pulled her car up next to a San Franciscan and asked:

"How far is it to Market Street?"

The San Franciscan considered it for a moment, and then told the woman:

"The way you're going, it's about twenty-four thousand miles."

暗誦例題 25.

A man went to his doctor for a checkup and the doctor told him:

"I'm afraid I must operate immediately."

"But I feel fine!" said the man.

"I'm sorry," said the doctor, "but I just checked you and you must have this operation. It will be very difficult to

perform, and it will cost you fifty thousand dollars."
"But I don't have that much money," said the man.
"That's all right," answered the doctor,
"you don't have to pay it all at once. You can pay it
in installments, paying a little every month."
"Oh," replied the man, "like you're buying a car."
"Yes, I am," said the doctor.

暗誦例題 26.

Two men rented a rowboat and went fishing in a lake. They were catching fish after fish, and had almost six dozens by the end of the afternoon. One man said to the other, "Why don't we come back to the very same place tomorrow?"

"Good idea," his friend answered.

So the first man took a marker, and drew an X on the bottom of the boat.

"Don't be stupid!" the friend said.

"How do you know that we'll get the same boat tomorrow?"

暗誦例題 27.

At a party the president of a stock brokerage company approached somewhat dejected looking man.

"Pardon me, aren't you Mr. Bush?"

"Yes, I am, and who may I ask are you?"

"I'm Gates of OK securities."

"Oh yes, I believe I've met you sometime before."

For a while the two talked about this and that. Then finally Mr. Gates changed the subject.

"By the way, is it true that you say you have over a million
dollars worth of stocks."

"Yes, you're well informed. I guess that my present stocks are worth about a million," replied Mr. Bush.
"Would you mind telling me how much you began with and how you invested it ?" asked Mr. Gates curiously.
"Yes, I will tell you. I inherited three million from my father, and then invested everything just like your company advised me to."

暗誦例題 28.
When asked what he planed to give his wife for her birthday, Mr. Johnson answered:
"Last year I gave her a pearl necklace and an alligator-skin bag, so this year I guess I give her a diamond ring and maybe a mink coat."
"Are you joking? You've been married for twenty years, and you mean to say you're still giving her an expensive stuff like that?"
"Not at all. I've never gone in for expensive gifts."
"Yeah.. but for the price of a diamond ring and a mink coat, it would be cheaper and more practical to buy her a car, wouldn't it?" said the friend in amazement.
Mr. Johnson winked as he answered:
"Yeah, but they don't make imitation cars."

暗誦例題 29.
Mr. Stevenson was about to go on a business trip. Like many experienced travelers, he took out a one-time flight insurance policy when he checked in at the airport. The policy he chose cost 1 dollar, and the payer's beneficiary was a million dollars if he died. Later, in his seat on the plane already high in the sky, he had a cup of coffee.

As he finished his coffee, when he found his fortune of the day written inside on the bottom of his paper cup. It said "your recent investment will bring back returns a million times what you pay.

暗誦例題 30.

A tourist making his first trip abroad was very nervous, and was unable to get any sleep on the plane. By the time he found all his baggage and reached the customs counter, he was a sorry sight. The customs officer asked routinely:

"Whisky, bourbon, vodka?"

The frustrated tourist replied:

"Well, thank you for the offer, but I am a bit tired and
still have a long way to go. But if you have any tea,
I'll take some."

暗誦例題 31.

A lively group of four middle-aged women boarded a train and took seats in the same compartment with never breaking the clatter. When the conductor came around to check their tickets, one of the women handed him four tickets. The conductor looked very surprised:

"Madam, your tickets are for New York. This train is headed
for Chicago."

The woman looked at her companions and then turned to the conductor.

"Well, there's no use telling me that. Tell the engineer."

暗誦例題 32.

A budget minded traveler was delighted when he found an inn on the outskirts of Los Angels with very inexpensive rates. He could hardly believe the sign outside which advertised rooms starting at twelve dollars. But next morning he looked miserable when he came to the desk and complained:

"What an awful room that was! All the night mice were going around. I didn't get a wink of sleep."

The man at the desk looked a bit surprised and asked:

"Did you stay in the twelve dollars room or the twenty dollars room?"

"I stayed in the twelve dollars room."

"Well then, those were not mice. We have rats in the twenty dollars room."

暗誦例題33.

A certain San Francisco restaurant became very popular recently after hanging an attractive sign in the front window, which read: "Fast and courteous self-service."

暗誦例題34.

Two men were having dinner in a hotel restaurant.

"Hey, why do you always wash your spoon in a finger bowl?"

"A Habit!" he said. "If I didn't wash it, I would get grease in all of my pocket, wouldn't I?"

暗誦例題35.

Two company executives were talking on a Monday lunch break.

"I'm exhausted. I took my wife to a department store for shopping yesterday."

"Really? So did I. Why is it that when it comes to shopping, a woman doesn't care how long she keeps her husband waiting?"

"But lately I have a great technique that I use when I get tired of waiting."

"Oh, what's that?"

"I just find some young salesgirl and start a conversation with her. Then before you know it, my wife appears out of nowhere and says, 'Come on, let's go!'"

暗誦例題 36.

On a night of a play known for sexually provocative scenes, a young boy sat for himself in a royal box. Shocked and a bit concerned, the woman in the next box called over:

"Young man, whose ticket do you come with tonight?"

"My dad's."

"My, where is your father tonight?"

"Oh, he is at home. I'll bet he is searching the whole house right now looking for this ticket."

暗誦例題 37.

A group of men were enjoying a porker game. One of them made a comment.

"Someday I would like to go to Las Vegas to make a fortune."

"You'd better forget about that," replied another. "I've never heard of anyone who came back from that place as winner."

"Yeah," added another, "they all come back saying what a good time they had, but their wallets are always empty."

Then the third man said:

"Well, I heard about someone recently who came back with a more expensive set of wheels than he went with."

"I don't believe it," said one of the others.

"It's true. He went there in a fifteen thousand dollar Toyota and came back in a bus worth hundred thousand dollars."

暗誦例題38.

A tourist visiting America got into a taxi in a small town. He was shocked, however, when his driver went through a red light.
　"Why didn't you stop at that signal?" he asked.
　"Because my bother never stops at red lights, and he has never had an accident yet," explained the driver, as he ran through three more red lights.
But when he reached a green light, he suddenly put on the breaks.
　"Hey, why do you stop at a green light. That's backward, isn't it? Driving through red lights and stopping at greens?"
The driver looked in the rearview mirror and explained:
　"I thought I just told you. What would happen if my brother came along and saw the red light and came driving through this intersection?"

暗誦例題39.

The owner of a gas station was about to go on a trip. He told a new attendant he had just hired to take over the station.
　"Will you fill up my car with gas?"
A little later, the owner came back and asked:
　"What's going on in here? I thought I told you to fill up my car."
The new attendant looked apologetic:
　"I did fill it up, sir. But when I opened the door, it all ran out again."

暗誦例題40.

Three men in high sprits held a taxi and climbed in. As they roll, they laughed and talked on about drinking and women. Soon the driver turned around and grumbled:

"How noisy bunch you are!"
The way he said was so gruff that it spoiled the fun mood of the drunks and they fell silent
   "In twenty years as driver, I've never heard of noisier bunch
      of passengers than you"
Then one of the man asked:
   "What kind of car have you been driving in the past
      twenty years?
Without looking back, the driver said dryly:
   "A hearse"

暗誦例題 41.

A conversation overheard in a hotel lobby:
A woman said,
   "No way! There's no way you put me in here!"
   "But madam..."
   "I paid a hundred fifty dollars for a room this night."
   "Of course, I understand that, madam."
   "Then, why are you trying to put me in a room like this?
   There's no furniture to speak of, no bath, no toilet. What do
   you think I am? Some country bumpkin that you can make
   fool of?"
   "But madam, this is not your room. This is the elevator."

暗誦例題 42.

"Excuse me, how much will it cost to stay here for one week?"
   a man asked at the front desk.
"Well, let me see now. I don't think we've ever had anyone stay with
   us that long."

暗誦例題 43.

A woman who had ordered a fish dish at a restaurant waited patiently for her order. No matter how long she waited, though, her order didn't come. At last her patient ran out, and she called over the waiter.
　"When will my order be ready?"
　"It will be ready in just a few minutes, ma'am."
　"Is that so?" said the woman, obviously unpleased.
　"Would you ask them what kind of bate they need to catch it?"

暗誦例題 44.

A New York restaurateur went all the way to Paris to hire a first class chef. Before long this chef had completely revised the menu with an array of new dishes including twelve varieties of soup alone. As a result the restaurant soon became a popular haunt for the city's gourmets. The owner's wife was thrilled by the new reputation.
　"Dear, what a success! I've never dreamt that this restaurant
　could become so popular."
　"Yeah, even I have to admit it. I underestimated the skills of
　a true first class Parisian chef."
　The owner smiled as he explained,
　"I mean, who could have thought that you could
　serve the same soup by seventeen different names without
　anybody realizing it?"

暗誦例題 45.

A man entered a somewhat elegant restaurant. The first thing he did, however, when he sat down at his table was to pick up a napkin and tuck it into his collar like a babe. Upset by such an unsavory guest, the manager called over one of the waiters.

"This is not just an everyday restaurant. We have our pride to maintain as the first class place. Find some tactful way to get that fool to put his napkin down on his lap."
Showing no hesitation at all with this rather delicate assignment, the waiter went straight over to the man and asked casually:
"Sir, would you like a shave or haircut?"

暗誦例題 46.

A daughter of a rich Middle East oil baron was showing off her diamond she had bought recently in New York to a friend. The conversation, however, soon turned to the proper pronunciation of an English word 'diamond.' The two happened to be walking past a jewelry shop at that time. The friend suggested:
"Well, why don't we go in here and ask the owner of the shop?"
Inside the shop the woman showed her ring to the owner and asked:
"Do you call this a /dáimənd/ or a /dáiəmənd/ ?"
The owner held the ring up to the light and examined it closely.
"Madam, in our business, this is referred to as cut glass."

暗誦例題 47.

A lavishly dressed middle-aged woman entered a fur shop.
"Well, Mrs. Jones, how nice to see you! What brings you in here today?"
"The bill for the coat I bought the other week arrived yesterday, and I came to take care of it."
"My, you need not come so soon," said the shop owner politely.
"Here you are. The check for the exact amount."
"Why, thank you. Oh my, this bill must have gotten wet. It's terribly stained. It must be a mailman's fault for letting it get rained on."

"Oh, no, it wasn't that at all," said the woman with no sign of emotion. "This was just my husband's tears."

暗誦例題 48.
At a high society party, a stranger approached a refined looking woman and struck up a conversation. But several times he cut the conversation short to go and get another serving of food and drink, which he quickly devoured. The woman warned him:
"You know, Mr. Carter, if you eat like that at one of these parties, you soon get a reputation as being a glutton."
"Oh, don't worry about me," he replied, "I've been telling them I am getting the food for you."

暗誦例題 49.
A politician famous for his womanizing had his sights on a certain actress. He telephoned her one day to say:
"For your birthday tomorrow, I'm going to send you a bouquet of the finest roses money can buy, one for each year."
The actress was delighted by his thoughtfulness. Knowing her real age to be thirty-one, the politician intentionally told his florist to deliver a bouquet of twenty-five of his most expensive roses. When he showed up at the actress's apartment next day, however, he was coldly turned down at the door. Disappointed and baffled, he called the florist and asked:
"Did you send the roses I ordered yesterday?"
"Of course we did, sir."
"And were they twenty-five of them like I specified?"
"Yes, sir. As a matter of fact, in appreciation of your continuing patronage, I even added extra ten."

暗誦例題 50.

A pilot was forced to make a crash landing in a desert. For days he walked in search of some trace of civilization. At last his canteen was empty, and he was dying of thirst. Then, out of nowhere appeared a single peddler:

"Sir, would you like a necktie?"

"A necktie? What're you saying? Can't you see I am dying of thirst? Don't you have any water?"

"Sorry I have no water, but these neckties are very cheap."

"I don't need a necktie."

The necktie peddler left, and once again the pilot began to crawl across the sand. Then suddenly, like a mirage, a big high-class restaurant appeared in front of him. The pilot was sure he was saved at last:

"Water! I need water! Let me in!" he pleaded, collapsing at the feet of the door man.

The door man, however, looked down and said coldly:

"I can't let you in here without a necktie."

● 文章まるごと暗誦のすすめ

いかがでしたか？　全部制覇するにはかなりの時間と苦労と集中力を必要としたことでしょう。なかなか一気にとはいかなかったと思います。本当にご苦労さまでした。

安定した暗誦ができるまで取り組まれた方はこれでほぼ半永久的にこれらのパンチ・ラインを脳裏に刻んでおくことができているはずです。

たとえ3日後、1か月後、1年後、10年後になかなか思い出すことができなくとも、標準メモ程度のメモさえあれば、不思議なぐらいスラスラと再構成ができる自分に驚かれることでしょう。

また、本文やメモがなくとも少し時間をかければ、一字一句元の文のとおりとはいかないまでも、小話の内容が再構成できるはずです。
　そして多くの人の場合、それが心の中で知らないうちに熟成・発展していて、より洗練されたかたちや、新たな創作が加わったかたちに生まれかわって湧き出してくることでしょう。つまり小話が自分の血肉の一部となるわけです。
　それこそが、
── あるがままのあなたの英語 ──
なのです。
　いずれにせよ、文章まるごと身につける。これが実際にできるようになるとその結果にたいへん満足できるものです。
　もしもそうでなかったとしても、有名な文章などを最初から最後までほとんど何も見ずに（メモ程度のものだけで）すらすら言えるようになれたら、それだけでも本当に楽しいことだと思いませんか？
　少しずつでいいですから、
── 文章まるごと身につける ──
ことに近づいていく。これを楽しみにすることができれば、語学を明らめることに一歩でも近づくことができるものと信じます。
　「明らめ」への人それぞれの「歩み」において人は人それぞれの「主体性」を育むことができます。暗誦がこだわりなく楽しくなったときに、あなたはあなたの英語と一体となり、「自分の英語をあるがまま」に受け入れることができ、
── 暗誦は主体性（自由）の追求 ──
となるのです。

付録　マルコムXのスピーチの暗誦例

マルコムXのスピーチ "More African than American"（Detroit, 14th February 1965）の一部分を暗誦の例としてとりあげてみました。後のメモを補助にして練習すれば、いつの間にかメモなしで簡単に暗誦できるようになれます。

メモは第4章で説明した規準におおむね沿っていますが、覚えやすさを考慮して多少規準と違う部分もあります。メモはあくまでも一例です。自分に合わなければ、自由に工夫・修正して下さい。

第2章を読まれた方は、このスピーチの"行間のメッセージ"を楽しみつつ、暗誦を試みることができると思います。

Why should the black man in America concern himself since he's been away from the African continent for three or four hundred years? Why should we concern ourselves? What impact does what happens to them have upon us? Number one, you have to realize that up until 1959 Africa was dominated by the colonial powers. Having complete control over Africa, the colonial powers of Europe projected the image of Africa negatively. They always project Africa in a negative light: jungle savages, cannibals, nothing civilized. Why then, naturally it was so negative that it was negative to you and me, and you and I began to hate it. We didn't want anybody telling us anything about Africa, much less calling us Africans. In hating Africa and in hating the Africans, we ended up hating ourselves, without even realizing it. Because you can't hate the roots of a tree, and not hate the tree. You can't hate your origin, and not end up hating yourself. You can't hate Africa and not hate yourself.

You show me one of these people over here who has been thoroughly brainwashed and has a negative attitude toward Africa, and I'll show you one who has a negative attitude toward himself. You can't have a positive attitude toward yourself and a negative attitude toward Africa at the same time. To the same degree that your understanding of and attitude toward Africa becomes positive, you'll find that your understanding of and your attitude toward yourself will also become positive. And this is what the white man knows. So they very skillfully make you and me hate our African identity, our African characteristics.

You know yourself that we have been a people who hated our African characteristics. We hated our heads, we hated the shape of our nose, we wanted one of those long doglike noses, you know; we hated the color of our skin, hated the blood of Africa that was in our veins. And in hating our features and our skin and our blood, why, we had to end up hating ourselves. And we hated ourselves. Our color became to us a chain — we felt that it was holding us back; our color became to us like a prison which we felt was keeping us confined, not letting us go this way or that way. We felt that all of these restrictions were based solely upon our color, and the psychological reaction to that would have to be that as long as we felt imprisoned or chained or trapped by black skin, black features, and black blood, that skin and those features and that blood holding us back automatically had to become hateful to us. And it became hateful to us.

It made us feel inferior; it made us feel inadequate, made us feel helpless. And when we fell victims to this feeling of inadequacy or inferiority or helplessness, we turned to somebody else to show us the way. We didn't have confidence in another black man to show us the way, or black people to show us the way. In those days we didn't. We didn't think a black man could do anything except play some horns — you know, make some sound and make you happy with some songs and in that way. But in serious things, where our food, clothing, shelter, and education were concerned, we turned to the man. We never thought in terms of bringing these things into existence for ourselves, we never though in terms of doing things for ourselves. Because we felt helpless. What made us feel helpless was our hatred for ourselves. And our hatred for ourselves stemmed from our hatred for things African...

(MacArthur 1992:353-4)

暗誦メモ

　　　Why should ___ _____ ___ in _____ concern _____ since __'s been away from ___ _____ _____ for three or four hundred _____? Why should __ concern _____? What impact does what happens to ____ have upon __? Number one, ___ have to realize that up until 1959 _____ was dominated by ___ _____ _____. Having _____ control over _____, ___ _____ _____ of _____ projected ___ _____ of _____ negatively. ____ always project _____ in _ _____ _____: _____ _____, _____, no_____ _____. Why then, naturally __ was so _____ that __ was negative to ___ and __, and ___ and _ began to hate __. __ didn't want any____ telling __ any_____ about _____, much less calling __ _____. In hating _____, and in hating ___ _____, __ ended up hating _____, without even realizing __. Because ___ can't hate ___ _____ of _ ____, and not hate ___ ____. ___ can't hate ____ _____, and not end up hating _____. You can't hate _____ and not hate _____.

　　　___ show __ one of _____ _____ over here who has been _____ brainwashed and has _ _____ attitude toward _____, and _'ll show ___ one who has _ _____ attitude toward _____. ___ can't have _ _____ attitude toward _____ and _ _____ attitude toward _____ at ___ same ____. To ___ same _____ that ____ understanding of and attitude toward _____ becomes positive, ___'ll find that ____ understanding of and ____ attitude toward _____ will also become positive. And ____ is what ___ _____ ___ knows. So ____ ____ _____ make ___ and __ hate ___ _____ _____, ___ _____ _____.

　　　___ know _____ that __ have been _ _____ who hated ___

付録　マルコムXのスピーチの暗誦例　**189**

_____ _____. __ hated ___ _____, __ hated ___ _____ of ___ ____, __ wanted ___ of _____ ____ _____ _____, you know; __ hated ___ _____ of ___ ____, hated ___ _____ of _____ that was in ___ _____. And in hating ___ _____ and ___ ____ and ___ _____, why, __ had to end up hating _____. And __ hated _____. ___ _____ became to __ _ _____ ― __ felt that __ was holding __ back; ___ _____ became to __ like _ _____ which __ felt was keeping __ confined, not letting __ go ____ ___ or ____ ___. __ felt that all of _____ _____ were based solely upon ___ _____, and ___ _____ _____ to ____ would have to be that as long as __ felt imprisoned or chained or trapped by _____ ____, _____ _____, and _____ _____, ____ ____ and _____ _____ and ____ _____ holding __ back _____ had to become hateful to __. And __ became hateful to __.

__ made __ feel inferior; __ made __ feel inadequate, made __ feel helpless. And when __ fell victims to ____ _____ of _____ or _____ or _____, __ turned to _____ ____ to show __ ___ ___. __ didn't have confidence in _____ _____ ___ to show __ ___ ___, or _____ _____ to show __ ___ ___. In _____ days __ didn't. __didn't think _____ ___ could do _____ except play ____ _____ ― you know, make ____ _____ and make ___ happy with ____ _____ and in ____ ___. But in _____ _____, where ___ ____, _____, _____, and _____ were concerned, __ turned to ___ ___. __ never thought in _____ of bringing _____ _____ into _____ for _____, __ never thought in _____ of doing _____ for _____. Because we felt helpless. What made __ feel helpless was ___ _____ for _____. And ___ _____ for _____ stemmed from ___ _____ for _____ _____...

引用・参考文献

浅井基文（1993）『国連中心主義と日本国憲法』岩波書店.
石坂和夫他（1993）『国際理解教育事典』創友社.
井筒俊彦訳（1964）『コーラン』（上）（改版）岩波書店.
英文日本大百科事典編（1997）『ビジュアル　英語で読む日本国憲法』講談社.
岡本薫（1999）『国際交流・国際理解教育のための　国際化対応の重要ポイント』全日本社会教育連合会.
デビッド・ギャレン編（1993）『マルコムX最後の証言』（東郷茂彦監訳）扶桑社.
言語権研究会編（1999）『ことばへの権利』三元社.
上坂昇（1994）『キング牧師とマルコムX』講談社.
ジェイムズ・H．コーン（1996）『夢か悪夢か・キング牧師とマルコムX』（梶原寿訳）日本基督教団出版局.
片倉もとこ（1991）『イスラームの日常世界』岩波書店.
小杉泰（1994）『イスラームとは何か　その宗教・社会・文化』講談社.
小林善彦・樋口陽一編（1999）『人権は「普遍」なのか ── 世界人権宣言の50年とこれから ── 』（岩波ブックレットNO.480）岩波書店.
佐藤良明監修・径書房編集部編（1993）『マルコムXワールド』径書房.
猿谷要（2000）『歴史物語アフリカ系アメリカ人』朝日新聞社.
デーブ・スペクター（1990-1）「ジョーク」（各地での講演）.
辻内鏡人・中條献（1993）『キング牧師 ── 人種の平等と人間愛を求めて ── 』岩波書店.
津田幸男（1990）『英語支配の構造』第三書館.
津田幸男編著（1993）『英語支配への異論　異文化コミュニケーションと言語問題』第三書館.
飛田茂雄（1998）『アメリカ合衆国憲法を英文で読む　国民の権利はどう守られてきたか』中公新書.
中村廣治郎（1998）『イスラム教入門』岩波書店.
サミュエル・ハンチントン（2000）『文明の衝突と21世紀の日本』（鈴木主税訳）集英社新書.
ひろさちや（1988）『キリスト教とイスラム教 ── どう違うか50のQ＆A ── 』新潮社.
ジョージ・ブレイトマン編（1971）『いかなる手段をとろうとも ── マルコムX ── 』（長田衛訳）現代書館.
────（1993）『マルコムX・スピークス』（長田衛訳）第三書館.
本田創造（1991）『アメリカ黒人の歴史』岩波書店.
増井由紀美、Kathleen M. Dooley、Scott Rivco（1992）『実力派の英会話』旺文社.

山内昌之（1995）『イスラムとアメリカ』岩波書店.
――――（1998）『イスラームと国際政治 ―― 歴史から読む ―― 』岩波書店.
和田勝明（1999）『英語科における国際理解教育』（『英語教育』別冊Vol. 48 No.3）大修館書店.
Ali, Ahmed (Trans.) (1988). *Al-Qur'ān: a Contemporary Translation*. Rev. ed. Princeton University Press.
Breitman, George (Ed.)(1990). *Malcolm X Speaks: Selected Speeches and Statements*. Grove Weidenfeld.
―― (Ed.)(1992). *By Any Means Necessary: Malcolm X*. Pathfinder.
Brown, H. Douglas (1994). *Principles of Language and Teaching*. Prentice Hall Regents.
Clark, Steve (1992). *February 1965 The Final Speeches: Malcolm X*. Pathfinder.
Cone, James H. (1991). *Martin & Malcolm & America: a Dream or a Nightmare*. Orbis Books.
Haley, Alex, and Malcolm X (1965). *The Autobiography of Malcolm X*. Penguin Books Ltd.
Honda Katsuich (1993). *The Impoverished Spirit in Contemporary Japan*. Monthly Review Press.
Huntington, Samuel P. (1996). *The Clash of Civilizations and the Remaking of World Order*. Touchstone.
Karim, Imam Benjamin (Ed.)(1971). *The End of White World Supremacy: Four Speeches by Malcolm X*. Arcade Publishing.
MacArthur, Brian (Ed.)(1992) *The Penguin Book of Twentieth-Century*. Benguin Book Ltd.
Pathfinder Press (1990). *Malcolm X on Afro-American History*. 3rd ed. Pathfinder.
Pietsch, Jin (1998). *New York City Cab Driver's Joke Book*. Warner Books.
Washington, James M. (Ed)(1992). *I Have a Dream: Writings and Speeches That Changed the World*. Harper Collins.

ビデオカセット（DVD）

Malcolm X (1992). Prod. Marvin Worth and Spike Lee. Victor Company of Japan.
Malcolm X: Biography (1995). Prod. ABC News Productions. A&E Television Networks.
Malcolm X: His Own Story As It Really Happened (1972). Prod. Marvin Worth and Arnold Perl. Warner Bros.
Malcolm X: Make It Plain (1995). Prod. Orlando Bagwell. MPI Home Video.

The Life and Death of Malcolm X (1992). Simitar Entertainment, Inc.
The Speeches of Malcolm X (1997). MPI Home Video.

コンパクトディスク

Music and Dialogue from the Original Soundtrack of the Motion Picture: Malcolm X
 (1972). Prod. Marvin Worth and Arnold Perl. Warner Bros. Records Inc.

その他

『日本国憲法』
New Crown English Series New Edition 3 (1997(平成9)) 三省堂.
The Charter of the United Nations
The Constitution of the United States of America.
The Declaration of Independence of The United States of America.
The Universal Declaration of Human Rights.
Universal Declaration on Linguistic Rights.

■著者紹介

島田　将夫（しまだ　まさお）

　昭和36年3月　京都市生まれ
　平成4年度より福山大学に勤務
　平成6年度からは福山平成大学に勤務
　英語、英会話などを担当

吉村　雅仁（よしむら　まさひと）

　昭和36年7月　岡山市生まれ
　昭和62年度より新居浜工業高等専門学校に勤務
　平成元年度より福山大学に勤務
　平成12年より奈良教育大学に勤務
　英語科教育特論、国際理解教育特講などを担当

あきらめの英語
―― あるがままの国際理解教育 ――

2001年10月30日　初版第1刷発行

■著　者――島田　将夫／吉村　雅仁
■発行者――佐藤　正男
■発行所――株式会社 大学教育出版
　　　　　〒700-0951　岡山市田中124-101
　　　　　電話 (086) 244-1268　FAX (086) 246-0294
■印刷所――互恵印刷㈱
■製本所――日宝綜合製本㈱
■装　丁――ティーボーンデザイン事務所

Ⓒ Shimada Masao & Yoshimura Masahito 2001, Printed in Japan
"Jesus of the People" by Janet McKenzie
Ⓒ Janet McKenzie
Illustrative reproduction rights arranged
with Janet McKenzie, Island Pond, Vermont, U. S. A.
through Tuttle-Mori Agency, Inc., New York
検印省略　　落丁・乱丁本はお取り替えいたします。
無断で本書の一部または全部を複写・複製することは禁じられています。

ISBN4-88730-451-X